SHORT CARRIES
ESSAYS FROM ADIRONDACK LIFE

Elizabeth Folwell

Drive slippery. The roads are careful.
WINTER 2009, NORTH CREEK, NY

Copyright © 2009 Adirondack Life, Inc.

All rights reserved. No portion of this work may be reproduced in any form without the written permission of the publisher.

Published by Adirondack Life, Inc.
The Brick Church
12961 NY Route 9N
Jay, NY 12941
www.adirondacklife.com

Cover photo © Nancie Battaglia
Author photo © Nancie Battaglia

Design Kelly Hofschneider

Folwell, Elizabeth
Short Carries: Essays from *Adirondack Life*
Anthology of articles previously published in *Adirondack Life* magazine

Manufactured in the United States

10 9 8 7 6 5 4 3 2 1
ISBN 978-0-922595-38-9

INTRODUCTION 1

SHADES OF BLUE

Imagining the Adirondacks 1
Egypt's Doghouse 4
Wish You Were Here 7
Last Train from Tahawus 12
The Final Tally 16
Bubble, Bubble, Toil and Syrup 20
Chilling Out 25
A Little Night Music 28
Ned Buntline, or the Blighter of Blue Mountain Lake 31
Adirondack Eldorado 40
Radical Chicks 45
Straight Shooter 48
Sorry, Long Number 54
Why We Bagged It 57
Wild Life Refuge 63
Taking Stock 66
A Clue in Clay 69
Notes from a Small Place 72
A Noble Set 76
Percy's Back Pages 79
Leaving Church 82
Waste Watching 85
They Shoot Trees, Don't They? 88
Scorched Earth 91
If These Walls Could Talk 95
School's Out 99
Totally Rad 102
Profit and Loss 105

SHADES OF GREEN

Lessons from a Dead Loon 111
Seeing in the Dark 114
Night School 117
Paths of the Paddlers 120
Natural Limits 126
Fish Shtick 129
The Bird in the Hand 132
A Season Apart 136
Turning Turtle 139
Trouble Bruin? 142
Bob Tale 145
Mood Indigo 148
Woods Bound 151
If Wishes Were Fishes 154
Red Wolf or Red Herring? 157
Dog Daze 160
Shake a Tail Feather 163
Freezing Points 166
Blinded by the Light 169
The Blue Goose 172
The Color of Water 175
That Sinking Feeling 178
Gold Rush 181
The Drifters 184
Blood Sport 189
New Loon 193
Trust Company 199

—Introduction—

PROBABLY EVERYBODY THINKS they lived in a golden age. For me it's always seemed that the 1970s and the 1980s were something like that in the Adirondacks, a time when the old rhythms of the society were still intact but there was new blood on hand too that appreciated those rhythms, paid attention, bore a kind of witness to what would soon start to pass away as the Blue Line turned ever more into a vacationland. Betsy Folwell is one of the very finest of those witness-bearers, and she has carried her slightly wistful sense of the near Adirondack past into all the essays that make up this crystalline, light-filled collection—a collection, it almost goes without saying, that any Adirondack bookshelf will be naked without.

The stories she tells of her early years in the park—the caroling from the dump truck, the truly classic tale of running the Blue Mountain store—remind me strongly of life in greater North Creek when I arrived from away in my early twenties. She's able to capture with an easy turn of phrase the resilient, deep, tough culture that still marked these hills. Read the account of the ore train from Tahawus to see how easily she understands the calloused culture now passing into memory. And hence her assessment of what came later has real resonance: "I can't wander over to the diner now for a big glass of iced tea, all sweaty after mowing the lawn, but I can buy wedding presents in five locations if I take a shower first."

Yet she's no sentimentalist, not even a little: she knows that many of the old-timers were the first to start trekking off to Warrensburg for the McDonald's or Ti for the Wal-Mart, and she knows that though the party line has vanished, the public radio has been a nice replacement.

And she knows, too, what glory never left. Not just human glory, though that's the easiest thing to write about in small essays like these. More deeply, she understands the natural glory of the place, which has gotten steadily deeper—"there's more there out there," she writes, and indeed there is, the wilderness quietly erasing all trace of what came before, and replacing it with a different sort of sweetness. The loon, resurrected.

Her account of that world reminds me sometimes of John Burroughs, a century earlier and in the more pastoral Catskills of the lower Hudson but still written with the same almost bemused wonder. Burroughs—the most popular writer of any kind in America in his heyday—would have enjoyed dozens of these pieces. The parade of turtles, for instance (which with its numerous examples offers proof of just how many miles of the Adirondacks Betsy has driven and walked over the years). Or her account of the humble woodcock's sudden spring ecstasy, rocketing skyward "like a water balloon from a slingshot" till he's reduced to "sound and sensed motion, formless."

Which brings us, by the way, to the heart of the matter. Folwell is as sweet a writer as you could wish. Her observations are wise, her humor earthy and quick, but it's her ability to bend a phrase that counts in the end. An ability that—strangely or maybe not—has flourished in the years since she's gone blind. Here's a description from "Blinded by the Light," when she was down to one eye and cherishing every sight: "The best summer days are those glowing ones, when all disheveled nature stands out in brilliant gilt-edged isolation, when the longest, widest vistas are as blowtorch sharp as the silver-burnished blueberries at your feet. The scales of a red pine tree aren't merely brown in this light, they're umber, rust and raw sienna in distinct oblong plaques."

Or this, from a couple of years later when the light had blinked out entirely: "On the edge of my field the forest posed a jumble of intensity, blood red, sunflower yellow, pumpkin orange. Behind the showoffs, the hemlock, spruce and balsam stood, patient and green, waiting for what comes next. The hardwoods were nervous in a wind, their leaves flipping and rustling, and finally drifting to the ground."

That's fall, and that's writing—"patient and green, waiting for what comes next."

Betsy Folwell has spent much of her life nurturing writers new and old—editing, connecting. She helped midwife the Adirondack Center for Writing, which has brought dozens of writers up to the light. And she's been essential in the daily life of the Adirondacks too—helping maintain its premier magazine at a high level, editing the best guidebooks to the park. She is such a force, so deeply ingrained in this place, that it's almost easy to overlook her single greatest talent, her own writing. What a pleasure to have this book, so we can renew our appreciation of it regularly. —BILL MCKIBBEN, *Middlebury College*

Imagining the Adirondacks
*She found her place by triangulation
—the points were Racine, India, Blue
Mountain Lake*

ONE OF THREE family vacations took us to my uncle's camp in the Finger Lakes, an eighteen-hour drive from home. I remember two things about the trip: being carsick and being carried up some hill to admire the view. My mother pointed east and said, "The foothills of the blah-blah-blah." "Foothills" stuck in my six-year-old mind; I wondered if they had toenails.

Having been favorably introduced to ferns, moss and big trees, I spent the next five years of my life trying to make a wilderness out of Racine, Wisconsin, population 85,000. This was not quite as far-fetched as it sounds—near our house was Lake Michigan and a narrow strip of raw land that held raccoons, possums, rabbits, ring-necked pheasants, ducks, crows, frogs and salamanders. Carp as big as cocker spaniels spawned in the shallows, and once a creepy dead sturgeon washed up on the shore.

I found an old trap in our basement, which also had a rifle range. For one winter when I was in third grade, I tended my trapline. I could barely pull the jaws apart, but I thought maybe

I'd catch a mink or a weasel even though I had never really seen one. I'm pretty sure Uncle Dick sprang the trap every night when he got home from the factory because I never got anything and I still had to set the trap every day. Uncle Dick was better acquainted with the more prominent residents of my lake bank, mostly big black Norway rats.

At eighteen, with $1,500 from my grandmother, I bought my own wilderness, 160 acres in northwest Ontario. It was flat and scrubby, had been burned over in the thirties, but close by were ponds, rivers and beautiful places like Lake Despair, just gray rocks and blue water. One night while visiting George Hughes, timber cruiser, fur trader, wild rice broker and raging alcoholic, I saw two moose and heard the northern lights. As silver and green circled the sky, they hissed and sizzled. I asked George and he indicated that this kind of thing happened all the time, if you only paid attention. I believe it was him, not the whiskey talking.

The next summer, some girlfriends and I headed east for a week. We climbed Mount Monadnock, in New Hampshire, hands and knees over rocks and blowdown. I was wild with joy. When we emerged scuffed and sweaty on top, there were hundreds there too, from Cub Scouts to grannies. That there was an easier route tarnished the experience just a little, but not the memory.

I first heard somebody mention the Adirondacks when I was in India, of all places. Joanne, a schoolteacher working with me at an educational center, recounted an ordeal of getting lost on Vanderwhacker Mountain. The Indian civil servants hearing the tale all nodded at the end and muttered, "Yes, yes, very awesome, Vanderwhacker Mountain." Later, when I saw the Himalayas face-to-face I realized the Indians' sympathy for Joanne's plight had to do with their idea of mountains, the homes of gods and goddesses, lost in clouds.

I moved east for good fourteen years ago. From the top floor of the building where I worked in Canton, I squinted, seeing the Adirondacks even though what was really out there was just treetops and farm fields. One frigid morning we tried to penetrate the Blue Line, but car trouble turned us back.

In 1976 I could not believe my good fortune to get a job in Blue Mountain Lake and live in the place I had so long imagined but only recently put a name to. I devoured the countryside from Conifer to Keeseville, ate the scenery with a spoon. No detail was too small. Occasionally there were (and still are) those freeze-frame moments when time just stops and understanding is complete. Once from Castle Rock, I saw below an osprey catch a fish; above, a red-tailed hawk caught a thermal and spiraled to infinity. From an upstairs window, in the moonlight, I saw a red fox make perfect tracks in the snow. While fishing with handlines, I saw the white birches become the warp, the leaves and sky the weft, and the wind wove the reflection into a perfect overshot coverlet.

Jean Wilson, a gifted artist who lived and died in town, painted picture after picture of Blue Mountain, from shocking pink to lavender to chartreuse to the more expected forest green and brown. I thought she was crazy, and then one November day, Blue Mountain looked like nothing so much as the gray coat of an old whitetail buck.

Talking to Art, whose life began with this century, I learned he too had seen fleeting moments of beauty and clarity. Looking at the Hudson River, I can hear Gerard's stories of river drives. You can touch the past here, the corners of a vista are held down with other people's memories. Most of us will never see a lynx or moose, but that doesn't stop us from dreaming about them.

All of us, whether we stay here or just visit, color the landscape with our own crayons. For some, imagining the Adirondacks has to do with notions of living an independent life, distinct from urban fears and suburban constraints. For others, imagining the Adirondacks means manly dreams about the big one that didn't get away and days well spent in the woods. For me, in imagining the Adirondacks I have to borrow from John Muir, who wrote that "going to the mountains is going home."

—MAY/JUNE 1989

Egypt's Doghouse
The sum of all changes and the balance of a community

A HUNDRED TIMES I've passed the white farmhouse with the fine front porch on a certain road less traveled. It's not the massive maple in the front yard or the well-sweep to the side that fascinates me, but the doghouse just to the right of the front door. Over the doghouse's door, in five-inch block letters is the word "EGYPT."

For a dozen years Egypt's doghouse has been an absolute, a constant, yet I've never seen Egypt gazing sphinxlike, her paws pointing south from her home. So I've pictured her as a saluki, with slim hips, silky ears and soulful eyes, or maybe as a spotted basenji with wrinkled brow and curly tail. Really, though, she's probably a country mutt, daughter of a hound named "Little Egypt," who serenaded coon hunters in the night.

Thinking about Egypt and her doghouse has occupied me for hours on the Northway, the way other people sing along with the radio or hold lucid arguments with themselves. That is, until the cozy world I had created with the sum of sixty-mile-an-hour glimpses came to pieces.

One morning Egypt's doghouse was off the porch, plopped

in the yard. The hay from inside the house had been h͟a͟ swept onto the grass. I almost drove off the road. When ͟. ͟.͟.͟.͟u͟ a chance to adjust, I played the scenarios in my mind: Egypt had met a skunk; Egypt had rolled in the putrid remains of a dead bear; Egypt was dead.

So small changes hit a community. Patterns are familiar, comforting, and once you learn the ropes, you begin to belong. So we wave to passing cars and trucks almost as a reflex, each with our own signature style. So we know to wait at the one-lane bridges rather than barge blindly across. So we turn out when the fire siren blows, even if the house aflame belongs to a ... *Democrat*. So we take local businesses for granted—the gas station that opens in the middle of the night for an emergency fill-up, the diner that makes a piecrust more delicate than the trendiest French pastry.

There used to be in our town a real general store, with spare chimneys for kerosene lamps, fresh meats and credit for anyone who asked. The proprietor cheerfully cashed paychecks on the weekends, only to watch that money migrate to other registers 30 miles away where the Campbell's soup was a nickel cheaper. It broke his heart and eventually his bank account. A generation ago our town, like so many others, supported more year-round businesses than it does today.

Something new and strange to me is afoot. The real-estate market first nudged, then shoved prices upwards, so some business people naturally chose to sell rather than pursue the few dollars that would only make them old before their time. But, with those modest changes, I wonder if the town didn't get gentrified before we had the chance to become gentry. I can't wander over to the diner now for a big glass of iced tea, all sweaty after mowing the lawn, but I can buy wedding presents in five locations if I take a shower first. Oh, I know the community benefits from any enterprise, if sales tax is collected the local folks get hired, but without these meeting places we draw more and more within ourselves and forget the casual pleasures of country commerce. We might as well be in our air-conditioned town houses thumbing through the catalogs.

The real-estate market has pushed some prices to levels

where no ordinary country business could meet the mortgage, pay the utilities and make a living. I'm not sure who—tourist or resident—needs another Candlemill Corner or famous-label-but-made-offshore outlet. The urge for many new country businesses is to clone Vermont or Connecticut, which just doesn't set right in these craggy woods.

I wish I did have the answer that would bring full and rewarding employment here and keep housing costs within reach. The raw materials that built the original Adirondack economy—the minerals and lumber—are not as competitive as they once were, in this new worldwide economy. The state-sponsored service industries such as prisons and intermediate care facilities can boost a local economy, but there's a finite limit to how many can be built, politics to play, and besides, the best jobs go to trained people from elsewhere who have come through the ranks.

The next time by Egypt's doghouse I noticed a fresh coat of paint on the porch. It was the march of time that sent Egypt into exile. But the good news is Egypt's doghouse is back where it belongs today. I wish I could say the same for Bump Callahan's store.

—SEPTEMBER/OCTOBER 1989

Wish You Were Here
Hand-tinted memories from Standard Supply

FOR FIVE YEARS the Standard Supply Company in Otter Lake (population 110) has manufactured and distributed all the souvenirs—postcards, pennants, balsam pillows—associated with a kinder, gentler Adirondacks. Behind the white frame storefront on Route 28, twelve miles south of Old Forge, three generations of the Norton family have crafted a business tradition untouched by changing times, screen-printing woodsy scenes, assembling photo albums, cutting out lawn ornaments, sewing felt pennants and publishing postcards commemorating communities from McKeever to Saranac Inn, Lake Placid to Lake George. For Standard Supply the graceful symbols of a summer vacation—the sprig of pine, the Indian maiden, the stately buck—are as fresh today as they were years ago when the inks were wet.

Roscoe Norton came to Oneida County, just inside the Blue Line of the Adirondack Park, from Boonville in 1904 to develop a new town between the thriving New York Central rail line and Otter Lake. He bought a massive hotel, built a road that nearly circles the lake, sold lots, and encouraged his pharmacist brother, John, to join in the business adventure.

John discovered he preferred photography to pill-rolling and began Standard Photo Supply Company a few hundred yards from the hotel in 1914. He began documenting the steamboat lines, the resorts and the train stations of the Fulton Chain with a five-by-seven-inch Kodak view camera, with color postcards to be printed from his black-and-white prints, and the mainstay of Standard Supply's wholesale business was born.

A generation before color film, vibrant-hued cards were lithographed. John Norton's proofs were hand-colored to create pastel sunsets, autumn leaves or rooster tails behind speeding inboards. Nearly 600 different images were printed. Today the warehouse, connected to the store by a wooden walkway, is an orderly collection of hundreds of boxes, each with the scene and the stock number printed on the end. The revolving racks in the store hold dozens of pictures of long-defunct destinations in lively tints, as if you, too, could still enjoy an excursion on Sixth Lake's *Osprey* launch or ferry your Terraplane across Raquette Lake.

The vacationing public soon wanted more than just postcards as mementos of the summer, and the nostalgic scents of sweetgrass and balsam were the company's next venture. Baskets from the St. Regis Reservation on the St. Lawrence River came by rail for wholesale distribution. By the mid-twenties, Standard Supply had cornered the balsam market. Lumberjacks in nearby Alder Creek, Woodgate and elsewhere cut truckloads of fresh greens in spring and summer to Norton's specifications: stems were to be "no bigger around than a lead pencil," according to his daughter-in-law, Gloria Norton.

In the workshop next to the warehouse, the balsam was chopped in an ensilage cutter, then blown into the attic and gravity-fed to a first floor bin. When the bin was full, the process was repeated. This aeration dried the needles to prevent them from becoming moldy, yet they stayed moist enough to retain good scent. Cut balsam was sold by the pound, and as it dried, it shrank. "Customers who received what they thought was 'short weight' were none too happy," said Gloria. Drying the balsam before packaging helped overcome this problem.

Bags of balsam went by train to pillow manufacturers, to the St. Regis Indian Trading Company, in Hogansburg, and points south. One major New York City account bought tons of balsam from Standard Supply every year.

Printed pillow tops and mailers, tiny bags with address tags attached, grew out of this bulk balsam business. Marlene Norton, John's daughter, drew the scenes from her father's photographs, adding geometric trim, a rustic arch, a chipmunk, fawn or Indian brave. Poems and mottoes were purchased "from struggling writers in New York City," Gloria said. Marlene stretched the fabric over screens her brother John B. had made, then filled in the fabric with a type of varnish. "She poked out the screen, hole by hole," continued Gloria, and John G. Norton, the third of that name, added, "It took days to make one screen."

The average pillow design contained three to five colors, so each screen corresponded to a particular ink. Each design was available with tan or black cloth, in sizes from 5 ½ by 8 ½ inches to narrow neckrolls to 17 ½-by-22 ½-inch tops. Father and son printed each and every pillow after cutting the cloth. Gloria said her husband "used to come home at night, tired and aching, and tell me he'd run the squeegee 867 times over the screens." Drying racks went from floor to ceiling in the print shop. Winter was the time to replenish the inventory, so the woodstove's heat helped dry the inks. "During the winter of 1936, for example, 9,392 pillow tops were completed, plus 6,643 mailers," recounted Gloria.

Once the pillow tops, pennants and mailers were printed, they still needed finishing. "Marlene would sew after working in the store until eleven or twelve at night," Gloria said. A Union Special overlocking sewing machine used three different needles with contrasting color thread. As needles worked together, a blade trimmed the edges of the cloth. In later years, mailers and pennants were "farmed out to housewives who were paid by the piece for their work," she continued. The last pillow top was printed in 1964, just after John A. Norton's death. It was a process demanding two pairs of hands, and young John G. was just six at the time.

Wood products were added to the wholesale line in the 1930s.

Lawn ornaments, a far cry from today's "fat fannies" and acrylic-pile-covered sheep, were Art Moderne–inspired ducks, ruffed grouse, canoes and wind vanes. Plaques and photo albums were good sellers by the 1940s. For the albums, son John B. cut out place names with a jigsaw, then stained or varnished the plywood covers and bound the books. Black paper was for "Snapshots" books, white for "Guests" and colors for "Scraps" books.

Not all items were successful: winter souvenirs never found a strong market. For a year or so the Nortons manufactured screen-printed felt armbands to wear over ski parkas, touting Old Forge, Speculator and other winter sports centers. In the 1930s, they sold Meyer snowplows to a variety of customers including J. P. Morgan.

At the height of Standard Supply's commerce, after World War II to the early sixties, the company carried more than 8,000 gift and souvenir items. Not all were made in Otter Lake: bracelets, hats, ashtrays and dolls emblazoned with forest scenes and homey maxims came from coast to coast and overseas. Wholesale customers—camps, hotels, hospitals, gift shops—numbered in the hundreds, from the Lake Placid Club to the American Legion Mountain Camp near Tupper Lake and Saranac Inn. Despite cutthroat competition, "Nobody has the variety we do, and we cater to smaller shops. We encourage their smaller orders, understanding that they can't tie up lots of money for such a short season," said John.

Although the manufacturing was strictly a family project, college students helped with the retail sales through the sixties. Room and board were part of the deal, with rooms above the shop. Now, these rooms display the entire wholesale inventory in lieu of a catalog, and high-school students and housewives staff the store as father and son visit customers throughout the park.

Nine old sample cases are stored in the attic, large fold-out trunks with contents that proclaim "Adirondack Mountains" on every conceivable product. John A. and John B. Norton would lug these to prospective buyers and steady clients alike, spending days on the road. Gloria recalled that reaching H. F. Ellmer's hotel, on Twitchell Lake, involved taking the highway to Eagle Bay, the dirt road to Big Moose, the side road to the

Twitchell Lake dock, a boat across the lake, a climb up a long flight of stairs from the hotel dock to the lobby, all for "maybe a hundred dollars' worth of stuff."

Wholesale and retail business is good again, say the Nortons, thanks to a renaissance of interest in the Adirondacks. They now distribute perhaps 2,000 items, including topographic maps, with delivery to customers twice weekly in the summer. Balsam pillow tops, felt pennants and souvenirs are still available in the store. All the salesmen's notebooks, bills, checks and records dating back to 1921 (the records from the first seven years were destroyed by fire) are tucked away, as are the meticulously labeled and scrupulously cleaned silk screens. In the workshop where the screens are stored the calendar reads "1924," but there is not a flyspeck or watermark on the page. Said Gloria, "When I was cleaning, I came upon a box of celluloid dolls. My mother-in-law had made dresses out of crepe paper for each one. To me, they were so beautiful. That's another example of the kind of care they spent on small things."

John G. Norton, thirty-one, continues the business with his mother and father. When asked if he expects to be around to celebrate Standard Supply's 100th anniversary, he says with a smile, "Of course!"

—NOVEMBER/DECEMBER 1989

Last Train from Tahawus
The ore train from North River chugs into history

SOME CHILL MORNING around Thanksgiving time, before the sun's light hits the top of Santanoni, a score or so of railroad cars filled with powdery iron ore will head south from Tahawus for the last time. The train will cross the Opalescent River, skirt the Hudson, follow the Boreas, pass Vanderwhacker Creek, and, finally, parallel the Hudson on its twenty-mile route.

On many maps these tracks are labeled "Delaware and Hudson" and, parenthetically, "United States Government." Therein lies a tale of how the Adirondack Forest Preserve's constitutional protection was waived in the face of special needs during World War II. One of those special needs was for a steady, secure supply of titanium dioxide with which to make camouflage paint for tanks. In 1941 National Lead Company bought the lands of the former MacIntyre Ironworks to mine titanium to make that paint, and that paved the way for railroad tracks through the state lands with little argument from the legislature.

A frenzy of activity erupted in the woods north of Newcomb. A two-laned, eight-and-a-half-mile highway was built virtually overnight, and a high-power electric transmission line was strung from faraway Ticonderoga. The tension of the power lines was so great that the team of horses drawing the massive cable taut were once snapped backward through the air. The railroad line was chopped, blasted and scraped out of the wilderness by hundreds of gandy dancers at a price of $2.5 million, paid by the federal Defense Plant Corporation. That job took nearly three years. Hopes for the mine's success were high. A front-page story in the *New York Herald Tribune* in June 1942 proclaimed "Modern Frontier-Adventure Story Written in Completion of Tahawus Plant, Whole Village and Roadway in Single Year by Force of 1,500 Workers."

Now the two vast pits, some 600 feet deep, are full of emptiness. Though there are still abundant mineral reserves, the market for the mine's products has diminished. Thirty-one workers stay on, mopping up, down from the 450 employees needed a decade ago. The last titanium was sent south in the fall of 1982; for the past seven years, iron ore has been the mainstay of the business. This iron doesn't go into Chevys or frying pans: it's used in separating coal from the base rock in processing plants.

The Delaware and Hudson Railroad, now in bankruptcy proceedings, operated the Tahawus trains from the first days until 1983. NL, one of just two industries on the D&H tracks north of Saratoga Springs, then formed its own rail crew: engineer Larry Pratt, from Minerva; lead trackman Al LaRocque, also from Minerva; and the "pin puller," yardman Charley Stickney, from Newcomb. Larry, now a forty-two-year veteran with NL, had some guidance from D&H men in learning to manage a 150-ton locomotive, but he said that "any machinery just comes naturally to me."

Charley rides in the engine with Larry. Usually Al goes by car—today, a venerable Ford Crown Victoria smeared with black magnetite—to stop at each railroad crossing in case the automatic signals should fail. If necessary, Al can stop highway traffic as the train passes. All this railroad's switches are manual, and the man on the ground ahead can throw the switch to divert the train or set "torpedoes"—small explosive charges—

on the tracks to warn the engineer of trouble ahead. Train and car maintain radio contact during the five-hour round trip.

Every mile of the way is marked with a concrete post indicating the distance to North Creek and back to Sanford Lake. Near crossings, a "W" painted in a white diamond reminds the engineer to blow the whistle, which sounds like an incongruous trumpet as we glide past a beaver flow on the approach to an old Finch, Pruyn logging road.

"Once we reach Newcomb Hill, we can coast nearly thirteen miles," Larry says as he tests the brakes. Driving the massive train seems a surprisingly subtle choreography of throttles and levers as Larry scans the countryside. There are few wide vistas, lots of water, rocks and trees. "You've got to know your tracks, your hills, your ups and downs," he remarks as he makes a discreet adjustment in air pressure for the brakes. "The longer the train, the easier it is to run. There's more forward momentum, more braking power," he adds.

The straight sections of rail were installed in the forties and, even then, they were twenty-five years old. "Curves don't last but eight or nine years," Al says. Charley explains how weather affects the rails: in summer, "heat kink" is caused by expansion, and in winter "the tracks can contract and pull so hard that the bolts holding the iron to the ties get cut right off."

For track maintenance the crew uses special "geometry cars" that check the elevation and gauge within quarter-inches over the miles, and a "Sperry car" that tests rails ultrasonically for unseen flaws. After a storm, NL crews patrol the tracks for debris, such as downed trees, in a "highrailer," an ordinary pickup equipped to ride on the rails. When they hit a snag, the men cut the trees with chain saws and roll the logs off with peaveys.

Two years ago, at milepost 15 near the Northwoods Club Road, a rockslide shifted the tracks three full feet out of alignment. Since then, the locomotive drops the ore cars just north of the slide area and motors ahead to be sure the way is clear. Occasionally cars are left at this Stillwater siding rather than at the North River yard, but a special hazard exists here: "Hedgehogs eat the brake hoses," according to Larry.

Each hopper on this twenty-five-car train holds 100 tons of

iron. To bring the same load over the highways would require about 100 tractor-trailers. The 2,300-horsepower, V12 diesel locomotive (its guts as big as my living room) uses about 200 gallons of fuel for the round trip. Top speed is about twenty miles per hour, and at that rate, the front of the engine rocks rhythmically from side to side, clip-clopping as we pass over the alternating joints of the rails. Charley says, "It's common for the engine to run six months without shutting off." In the harsh winters at Tahawus, the locomotive idled in a heated shed. Unfortunately, keeping that locomotive warm won't be a worry anymore.

NL expects to close before the end of 1989, but will keep a skeleton crew on to reclaim the land. In August of this year the company spent nearly a million dollars to purchase the railroad right-of-way from the General Services Administration. Gordon Medema, general manager at NL, explains that "buying the railroad enhances the value of the property. A thirty- to fifty-year mineral deposit remains here, and perhaps the world market will improve to the point where NL or some other buyer would operate here again."

After the train passes the "roundhouse"—the North River General Store—wing-shape signs mark the yard limit where the full cars will be uncoupled to be picked up by a southbound D&H engine, and where empty cars wait for the trip north. By car, we head for coffee and hot sticky buns at the "station"—Smith's Restaurant in North Creek. Around the table, Al, Charley and Larry sit quietly. Their crows' feet and laugh-lines are caked with black magnetite dust, and their faces are set in the distant half-smile they save for the end of the road.

—NOVEMBER/DECEMBER 1989

The Final Tally
The century goes down for the count

APRIL 1, 1990, I'm told by some people in suitcoats, is not really the day we put salt in the sugar bowl and ask the butcher if he has pigs' feet. Instead, it's Census Day, when a half million people with clipboards begin probing our personal details and inquiring about the status of our household plumbing. In the Adirondacks, the distinction between native and newcomer will be temporarily overlooked—after all, our sheer numbers will determine how much money comes back to town in loans, grants and revenue sharing. Perhaps those of us who are of childbearing age but yet without children should arrange to borrow babes from other towns for that day when the strange late-model sedan pulls into the driveway.

The first census, 200 years ago, didn't need extra tots to justify federal expenditures in out-of-the-way places or more seats in Congress. George Washington knew he was first in war, first in peace, but he wasn't certain in just how many countrymen's hearts he was number one (and he needed to know—so he could tax them in order to pay for the Revolutionary War). I've read he was disappointed to learn that figure was less than four million.

Temporary U.S. marshals rode hundreds of miles to count heads in the vast counties that then included the North Country. In the farthest-flung reaches of Queensbury, what is now Igerna, I can picture the enumerator's surprise to find a two-story clapboard home with real float-glass windows, a brick chimney and sawn boards for the floors, rather than the usual hastily assembled shacks of young families trying to beat a living out of the stony ground. The information the government wanted wasn't much, just a thumbnail sketch of the household, and the time spent traveling from dooryard to dooryard was probably a hundred times longer than the official interview.

By 1840 the Adirondacks had been carved into the counties we recognize today, and the census taker's task was complicated by more people to see, more questions to ask. Marching across the lefthand page of each leather-bound, government-printed document was the legend "Free White Persons, Including Heads of Families." Slaves and free persons of color were counted, although their age categories were not the same five-year brackets as for white folks: slaves were noted in age cohorts that approximated their economic usefulness: child, youth, young adult, middle age and centenarian. Occupations were recorded in a column that asked for the "number of persons in each family employed in mining, agriculture, commerce, manufactures & trades, navigation of the oceans, learned professions and engineers."

Deaf, dumb, blind and insane white persons were counted, although the government felt no need to know just how old the idiots and sightless were. Scanning the Essex County census for 1840, it appears that families were large, parents were young and farming was virtually the only trade.

By 1880 Adirondack communities, riding the first great wave of European immigration, had grown considerably. In the town of Morehouse, in southern Hamilton County, many inhabitants had come from Prussia, Alsace, Hanover and Wurttemberg, while most Minerva residents had been born in Ireland or Canada. Life expectancy for white men and women was forty-two and forty-three, respectively.

The census takers found their way to many lumber camps, where they described the women's work as "keeping shanty," and the men's as "log choppers." The tanneries, mines and industries offered new occupations, and the growth of hotels led to lists of laundresses, bellboys, clerks, barbers, gardeners, bartenders and chambermaids where a generation ago only farmers had been. In perusing thousands of names, I ran across only one "gentleman"; he lived in Morehouse.

I can see the enumerator taking a deep breath before reading this question to the head of the house: "Is the person sick or temporarily disabled so as to be unable to attend to ordinary business or duties? If so, what is the sickness or disability?" In Minerva, the census taker found a woman suffering from dyspepsia and a man taken with "heart affliction." One day, rued I'm sure by the intrepid traveler, he found consecutive households with measles, whooping cough and diphtheria, adding real danger to an otherwise non–life-threatening job.

The names, written with handcarved nibs, give a clue to the hopes and aspirations of a growing country. Men were named after virtues and abstract principles, like Loyal, Justice, Christian, Freeman and Freeland, or heroes and mythic places, like Delos, Achilles, Fabius and Adolphus. Women's names resounded with poetry (Cellestia, Philecia, Mendamia, Alveretta) and, perhaps, even fiction, in the case of Novella, who lived in Benson.

The 1900 census pried even more into the lives of the people, although the concern over counting the unhealthy and handicapped gave way to curiosity over education and economic status. Narrow columns noted those who "can read," "can write" and "can speak English." For the first time, the government wanted to know who owned his or her own home and if it was free of mortgages. New occupations proliferated; Piseco had an electrician in 1900, although exactly what he did remains a mystery to me.

Analyzing or even copying the data compiled by the army of head-counters must have taken clerks years to assemble. I've read that nearly a decade passed before the 1880 census was published, despite the aid of a mechanical tallying machine. Even now it takes some work to make sense of the facts of life. In Hamilton County the population was 4,400 in 1910, had inched up to 4,700 by 1970 and just tipped 5,000 by 1980. Essex County showed the same pattern, while Franklin County lost residents over those seventy years. The rest of the state more than doubled in population during that time. What is significant, too, about those Adirondack counties is not only their lack of growth, but the high percentage of residents over sixty. Nearly a quarter of Hamilton County is what demographers call "aged." Where I live, in Blue Mountain Lake, the average resident is a dozen years older than his or her urban or suburban counterpart.

A hundred years from now, that bit of data may be tripped over by some well-meaning researcher, and the North Country of the 1990s might just be depicted as an exotic enclave of robust oldsters, not unlike remote valleys of the Caucasus where they all eat yogurt and live to be six score and more.

—MARCH/APRIL 1990

Bubble, Bubble, Toil and Syrup
North Country saps discover the sweet life

MAPLE SUGAR SEASON, that tentative time that's barely winter and not quite spring, announces itself at our place when the road, hard as concrete, turns to treacle overnight. Then we go upstairs in the barn to locate a ragtag stash of galvanized metal—buckets, covers, spiles and evaporator pan—that got buried behind the screen doors, cider press and skis of the preceding seasons. We've been backyard sugaring for fifteen years, operating from complete ignorance at first to a level of skill now commensurate with our still-primitive equipment.

Our first year in the North Country we tapped a whole hillside of trees, including a cherry and a dead maple. The neighbors came by to offer advice, shake their heads in disbelief or snicker. In self-defense we hung a bucket on the nearest power pole, filled it with creosote and told them it was a "wire tap." But, by golly, we actually did make real syrup from real maple sap from real maple trees, and it tasted just fine—even if it was as black as your Bean boot bottoms.

Sugaring weather is freezing nights and warmer days. The sap, stored in the roots all winter, makes its way upward to nourish the branches. The old-timers can tell you whether the sap is running just by sniffing the air. Of course, the best way is to check for yourself. Your backyard operation ought to have at least a half-dozen sugar maples one foot in diameter or larger, because you want to gather enough sap to warrant all the work of boiling off. Forty gallons of sap make one gallon of syrup, as a general rule, although the first run's ratio can be as sweet as 25:1.

You'll need a brace with a ⅝- or ⅞-inch bit; spiles with hooks (also known as spouts or taps), one for each bucket; covers; containers and a hammer. Tyros might want to mark 1 ½ inches on the bit with tape. You need to penetrate the bark when drilling into the tree, but you don't want to go too deeply into the sapwood. Drill at a slightly upward angle, and if there's deep snow, drill lower than waist-high. One season we had a terrific amount of snow on the ground, and as it melted the buckets got higher and higher until they were nearly above my head. I challenge you to try to remove such a bucket, brimming with two gallons of frigid liquid, without taking an impromptu shower.

Tap your trees on the south side first. Trees over sixteen inches in diameter can take an additional bucket or two. The canopy of the tree also indicates its sap-producing potential; bigger is better. A few taps are not harmful to the tree, but in succeeding years, don't drill near the scarred-over holes.

We use real sap buckets, some sixteen and some twenty-two quart, because we got them for free. You can use large cans, gallon milk jugs or whatever holds water. A good tree can produce more than two gallons of sap per bucket per day, and I prefer to empty the buckets just once a day. You don't have to use covers, but after a mouse took a fatal bellyflop into one of our buckets I became a convert. Besides, the sap is pretty diluted already — why boil off the rain, snow and sleet, too?

Pound the spiles in the holes. This step seems self-explanatory, but if you just bash them with a hammer the spiles get mangled and become harder to remove at the end of each season. Use a piece of scrap lumber to soften the blow, or get a cast metal spile-driver that fits right inside. At a couple of bucks, they're a good investment, and you'll only need one.

Once your buckets are hung on the maples, stand back and

listen to the syncopated plinking and plunking. Don't rhapsodize too long, though. You need to gather wood, rinse out a storage container, scour the evaporator pan and find a level spot to build your fire. We tap trees on a Thursday for a weekend boil. Sap can be stored for a day or two in a new or very clean garbage can; we pile snow around ours to keep it cold. If it freezes, it's actually beneficial, because the ice helps concentrate the sugar in the remaining sap. If your stored sap is gin-clear, it's still good. If it looks like imported beer, it's not. If it grows pink filmy stuff reminiscent of a Cyndi Lauper costume, pitch the batch and clean out your storage unit.

Our evaporator pan is two feet wide by three feet long and about ten inches deep, with two handles on the long sides so we can take it off the fire easily. The guys at a local shop charged us thirty-five dollars to fabricate it from sheet metal. The key is to find a pot that holds at least fifteen gallons and has a large surface area.

Our "arch," or firebox, is a fifty-five-gallon drum, cut down so the pan sits partway inside with two angle irons for bracing. The back has a hole for a stovepipe elbow, and the front has two handles so it can come right off for power-loading wood. A friend with an arc welder made it in exchange for a case of beer. You can use concrete blocks, firebricks, rocks or other materials to make a support for the pan that gives you at least sixteen inches underneath to build the fire.

We don't boil until we've got a batch of at least twenty-five gallons of sap. Start early in the day, check the wind direction and get the fire roaring. Have several buckets of sap ready to pour in the pan nanoseconds after you've placed it on the fire. Once, we made the mistake of preheating (someone else's) empty pan—the solder joints made cute little silver balls as all the seams opened wide. You want to have the pan as full as possible. Get the sap to a violent rolling boil and keep it there. This is harder than it sounds. As you add wood to the fire, the sap's temperature drops, and, of course, it cools off as you add more sap to the batch.

The pros avoid adding cold sap to a boiling batch, and you should, too. Preheat it in a metal bucket or stewpot on the back or side of your fire. The more cool sap you add the darker your finished product will be, as the already-made sugar gets burned. But it's nearly impossible to make extra-fancy light-amber syrup in a backyard setting anyway. Console yourself by saying the dark stuff has more character, more robust flavor.

When the liquid in your pan is low enough to fit in your largest kitchen pot (I use a twenty-five-quart canner), it's time to move the final stages indoors. If you're only using your kitchen stove for an hour or two, you probably won't steam off all the wallpaper or warp the window frames. You can burn an entire batch by not watching the pot, and you can also end up with granulated syrup if you wait too long. As the sap approaches syrup—sixty-six percent sugar—it has a nasty tendency to boil over. A bit of butter dropped in the pot tames the bubbles.

There are lots of scientific measures to tell when your product is finished. When maple syrup reaches seven degrees above the boiling point of water, it's done. But in order to be accurate, you need to calculate at what temperature water boils on the day you're sugaring since that varies with the barometric pressure. You can invest in a syrup (not a sap) hydrometer and familiarize yourself with the Brix scale, specific gravity and so forth. Or you can go the low-tech route that's only let us down once in a decade and a half: when the syrup "aprons" off the dipper, it's done. Our dipper is a plain little spatula. We hold it above the pan, out of the steam, and if the liquid hangs off the end in a sheet rather than dropping down in watery drips, it's syrup. You can taste it, too, after it cools a bit on a plate. If you like the flavor and viscosity—say, thirty-weight—proceed with canning.

Filtering the hot syrup is one of the trickier parts of the process. A real felt "witch's hat" filter is the best strainer, available from a maple supplier, but lots of layers of cheesecloth in a sieve will do in a pinch. Wet either fabric with hot water and wring it out first. Don't bother trying coffee filters, as the syrup is too thick to penetrate even when it's boiling hot. What you're filtering out is bits of visible detritus and also a by-product called niter or sugar sand. My guess is that most commercial syrup comes in metal cans so the consumer can't see the inevitable thin layer of suspended solids on the bottom. Your syrup will have some; just don't lavish it on the guests' pancakes. The run ends when the sap gets "buddy," as the old folks say. The sugar content gets depleted by the tree's renewed growth, shown in maroon buds. Pull your taps, clean them in hot water and let your buckets dry in the sun.

One year, when we were unemployed, we actually made enough syrup to sell. Usually, though, we use our own honey-thick syrup extravagantly at home in baked beans, brown bread, barbecue sauce and on ice cream. Occasionally, we give it to family and friends, provided they appreciate the hard work and good humor that goes into each jar.

—MARCH/APRIL 1990

Chilling Out
No flowers, no leaves, no bugs, no bees, No-vember

NOVEMBER IS HARD to love. Sure, there are advantages: shorter lines at the supermarket checkout, more parking spaces at the post office, no awakening birdsong at four a.m. Just before Labor Day, some of us may have been heard to say we can't wait to get the country back. But now that it's ours—and ours alone—we're not so sure we want it, warts and all. Every paradise has its price, though, and this one's final payment comes due this month, borne on raw winds and steely skies.

November's daylight hurries from dawn to dusk, as if there's so little left of the sun's warmth that it has to be parceled out in meager doses. There's no turning back, no more excuses: time to put on the snow tires, put away the canoe paddles. Winter's coming on.

November turns us into ants, even if we were born with grasshopper tendencies. Stashing, storing, working—squeezing every morsel of time out of the day is part of the season. The last bit of wood goes on the woodpile with the satisfying thunk of dry maple. This piece is for next year, we tell ourselves, knowing deep down that it'll come in with the melting snow from a March blizzard. The kerosene can's filled for the inevitable storm that brings down the power lines; the freezer's got an assortment of odd-shaped packets to provide a faint taste of summer when sleet beats on the windows.

Every fall I make a stab at fooling the march of time, to get one last meal out of the grudging ground. Sometimes the garden thrives, sort of, but mostly the plants remain spinsters because there aren't enough bees still at large to pollinate them. The dirt's not yet frozen, but the deer have ruled my garden for weeks, leaping over the fence like gazelles. They've mowed the kale, pulled up the carrots and daintily snipped the brussels sprouts off the stalks, leaving behind prehistoric-looking gray clubs.

The November woods are stripped bare, down to the basics of trunks and branches, roots and mud. There's no softness of leaf shapes to break up the powerful vertical sweep of trees, no frillery of green fern to disguise the starkness of boulder and brookside. The land's contours are drawn bold, as vivid as the brown lines on the topo maps. Colors are somber, monochromatic. Instead, textures stand out: the widewale corduroy of ash bark, the seamless suede of moss.

Even November's sounds are distilled to single repeated notes: the dry *tick-tick-tick* of beech leaves rattling in the wind, the peculiar coughing bark of a gray fox, the deep groan of a deadfall hung up high in another tree's crown. (No wonder the old-timers call them widow-makers—one good blow could bring them crashing down on an unsuspecting lumberjack.) Smells are subtle, too. The sweet scents of balsam and freshly cut grass, magnified by warm air, are gone, replaced by the dank musk of popple trees and decaying leaves.

Late fall is hunting season, not just for guys with guns but also for those of us who've left things out, lost things. These are the victims of summer's many distractions, now visible since the leaves are down. A hat shows up, trapped in the spikes of a hawthorn tree, a pair of gloves appears on an old stump, and the green garbage pail that a bear dragged into the swamp stands out among the red branches of dogwood.

This is the season for pancake suppers at the firehalls, election-night dinners in church basements, cake sales, bake sales, pizza sales, candy-bar sales, bazaars. Carbohydrate loading becomes a cultural necessity in preparing for winter. The holiday spirit is held together with flour, sugar and butter, rolled out in familiar patterns, baked in a moderate oven.

It's also the time for square dances with folks who know all the tunes from "Nellie Gray" to "The White Cockade," for watching the couples who glide as if they're on ball bearings, for dancing with the men who'll swing you so hard your feet—both feet—leave the floor. It's time for long nights of popcorn and poker, catching up with old friends and hearing the well-worn stories around a working woodstove.

Sometimes there are fluky days, so clear, so pure, so unbelievably warm with borrowed breezes from some tropic somewhere. But they're as rare as a loon's yodel on Thanksgiving Day. The pivot point comes with the first real snow, the one that sticks, when the season's balance tips from late fall to winter, for good.

—NOVEMBER/DECEMBER 1990

A Little Night Music
Getting in tune with the season

YOU CAN ALWAYS pretty much count on a white Christmas in the North Country, with all the right sounds and smells. But that instant of recognition that makes you understand this season is special, that appreciation sparked by some minor event—something discretely different from the ordinary stream of affairs—well, that's something you can't plan. And it doesn't always happen how and when you expect it to.

We went Christmas caroling through Blue Mountain Lake one frigid December eve, yowling songs from the back of a dump truck. This caroling expedition mushroomed all on its own. Our town's a little too spread out to make marching from door to door much of a jolly affair, and going from driveway to driveway, piling in and out of a bunch of cars, seemed to be an awful lot of work. An open-air truck would do for our expedition, but it would have to be a big one to fit everybody in. So with the luck of the season on our side, a driver volunteered, along with his brother-in-law's tandem-axle dump truck filled with bales of good hay. With great cheer we climbed up a ladder and piled into the dump box.

We were quite the mongrel choir. There were a few teenage boys (a surprise, since they were best known for perpetrating the kind of mischief that only life in a small town can inspire), a couple handfuls of younger kids, some parents and some older folks. Percentage-wise we represented about a quarter of the available humans within a twelve-mile radius. Maybe three or four of us could actually sing. The rest of us had no ability whatsoever.

Thundering down the road, we lustily crowed away to the trees and solitary passing cars. "Angels We Have Heard on High" lasted for a country mile as we dragged out the "Gloria" part. Early on, the little kids got bored with the singing and instead scuffled in the hay, stuffing it down each other's snowsuits. The teenagers were hoarse within minutes. But they all got back into the music when we stopped at houses where the families came out on their stoops to listen, bravely shivering in the night air.

At several places we didn't get much response. Maybe a porch light flashed, or the curtains momentarily parted. Or someone came to the back door, saw the truck, thought it was a late delivery of something and went back in.

We pulled into the driveway of one house, practically onto the front porch. Peering over the high sides of the box, we could see that the folks inside were watching TV, oblivious to all the racket outside. The diesel was throbbing, the exhaust stack's flapper was pinging and we were all howling so loudly we had to muffle our ears, but there was no glimmer of recognition from the cozy living room. And so the driver hit the air horn. And those two people levitated, but fast, out of their lounge chairs. They came to the window, smiled and waved—which was enough stimulus for us to launch into another tune at maximum volume; they disappeared.

As we headed up the highway it was slowly occurring to some of us that our audience probably couldn't hear us much over the truck's throaty idle, and some folks whose windows were considerably below the level of the dump box couldn't even see us. What we were doing started to seem sort of silly. No one said anything, but our singing got thin and quavery as we stood in a dispirited huddle, looking down at our feet.

The truck climbed the hill, downshifting loudly enough to wake the bears, to the last few places on the edge of town. At our final stop the driver turned off the truck, which is a risky thing to do in bitter air. The sudden quiet was like the slam of a door. Below us the village looked innocent and vulnerable; we half expected to see a Lionel engine go chugging past the firehall. We rallied for one last try on one of those simple Christmas lullabies, and when we stopped we could hear our echoes roll off the hillside. We were ready to beat a sheepish retreat, ready to forget about the whole thing.

But the lady of this house saw us, and heard us just fine. She came out to the truck with a platter heaped with homemade fudge. A score of mittened hands grabbed; we all gobbled. Someone had finally appreciated our foolishness. We couldn't help but be all choked up, emotionally and physically. That dose of warm, gooey chocolate made our throats clamp down tight. Another *fa-la-la-la-la* was out of the question.

As we trucked our way home, I remember thinking that so much of this season's energy is spent on picking the right gifts, and then worrying whether the people we've bought these things for will like them. But we might instead consider the measure of small gestures, delivered at the risk of their looking simple, things exchanged freely from the heart.

—NOVEMBER/DECEMBER 1991

Ned Buntline, or the Blighter of Blue Mountain Lake
The improbable life and times of Edward Z. C. Judson

"The life history of Col. Edward Zane Carroll Judson 'Ned Buntline' is more thrilling than romance, as his career, from boyhood to middle age, was a succession of adventures by land and sea; as a sportsman and angler in the then-primitive wilderness in the Adirondacks, as a midshipman in the Navy, a soldier in the Seminole war, the Mexican war, the four years of warfare between the North and the South and finally in the Indian Wars of the wild west." (From Life and Adventures of Ned Buntline *by Fred E. Pond ["Will Wildwood"], New York, 1919)*

"... a black-hearted toad ... a rank coward, an assassin, a seducer and a murderer ... with a face like a bladder of lard, almost goggle-eyed, humpbacked and red-headed." (From Private Life, Public Career and Real Character of That Odious Rascal Ned Buntline!! As developed by his conduct to his Past Wife, Present Wife and his Various Paramours! Completely lifting up the Veil and Unmasking to a Horror-

Stricken Community his Debaucheries, Adulteries, Revelries, Cruelties, Threats and Murders!!! *by Thomas V. Patterson, New York, 1849)*

The Adirondacks' first writer-in-residence, Edward Z. C. Judson, aka Ned Buntline, Edward Minturn, Charley Clewline, Reckless Ralph, Sherwood Stanley, Julia Edwards and Ethelbert the Wanderer, was a legend in his own mind. Published accounts of his real and imagined exploits fueled the tabloids of the mid-1800s: With a handful of fellow adventurers he plotted to annex Canada and was foiled in Quebec City; he fought in a dozen duels and led murderous mobs. He railed against obscene literature as he carried on numerous torrid love affairs, and spoke out for temperance with booze on his breath. He met a jack-of-all-trades from Iowa, William Cody, and catapulted him into fame as Buffalo Bill, thus creating the mythical Wild West that Americans swallowed hook, line and sinker.

Buntline cranked out no fewer than 150 serial romance novels during his half-century career, all about fallen angels, prodigal sons, devious foreigners, demure maidens and virtuous, red-blooded American men; his *The Mysteries and Miseries of New York* was a runaway best seller in 1847. He made a fortune from unabashed trash and rivers of saccharine.

Buntline left his mark on the howling Adirondack wilds in the years preceding the Civil War and paved the way for a generation of outdoor writers. He's the person who insisted that Clinch, or Tallow, Lake be called the more lyrical Blue Mountain Lake, and the first year-round road out of that territory was hewn in order to get Buntline's manuscripts to his publisher.

Buntline's tales of his experiences with rod and gun were among the first to describe the Adirondack woods and waters to a national audience; these hyperbolic he-man essays found their ways into respectable anthologies that included works by Nessmuk and fishing experts Charles F. Orvis and Seth Green.

His lurid accounts of shooting a pack of slavering wolves, hauling a twenty-four-pound salmon out of Blue Mountain Lake, clobbering a 300-pound buck with an oar while rowing in Eagle Lake and watching his English bulldog tree an entire family of panthers thrilled an eager public that wanted to revel vicariously in this new frontier. The subject of "The Big Buck of Blue Mountain," a story published in the late 1850s, was a near-mythical creature "so cunning as to baffle every hunter who tried to bring him down; so strong as to bear away more than one chance ball, which had touched, but failed to reach a vital part of him, and so fierce that none of our dogs could drive him to water, so foxy, too, in his nature that he fed in my fields at night …" City folks ate it up with a spoon.

It was a dark and stormy night when Buntline was born, one March 20. The year was either 1819, 1821 or 1823; accounts, including his own, vary. His father, an attorney in Stamford, New York, hoped that his son would follow in his footsteps, but Buntline preferred hunting and fishing to studying. He left home at an early age to join the Navy. Buntline wrote, "I had sailed around the world when I was eleven, was promoted to midshipman when I was thirteen." His years before the mast, roughly 1838 to 1842, provided him with great literary inspiration as well as with his nom de plume (a buntline is a rope used to haul up a square sail).

"Eating the Captain's Pig," his first published work, appeared in *Knickerbocker* magazine, in 1838. By the time he was twenty-one (or twenty-three or twenty-five), Buntline had enough backing and material to launch his own magazine, called, modestly enough, *Ned Buntline's Own*. At times an issue would contain a half-dozen serials written under assorted pen names, all by one and the same.

Although Buntline's writing career was launched to dazzling success, his marital fortunes weren't quite so sweet (he was widowed, married and divorced, and remarried in short order), and his political career was just as tempestuous (he was the leader of the xenophobic United Sons of America). Buntline's magazine, published out of Paducah, Kentucky, was a mouthpiece for his secret military order as much as it was a vehicle for his fiction. The group, with Buntline as its leader, gained the national spotlight with the infamous Astor Place Riots, in 1852, in which twenty-three people were killed and twenty-six wounded. Buntline was convicted of leading the riot, fined

$250 and sentenced to a year in jail.

Buntline was on the rebound in 1856 when he first saw the Adirondacks. Some say what drove him out of the city was the crashing failure of radical politics, while others suggest it was affairs of a more domestic demeanor, that he was avoiding his ex-wives. *The North Creek Journal* offered yet another explanation: "In '60, when he was known here, he was intermittently a hard drinker. He went, or was sent [by his publishers, Cauldwell, Southworth and Whitney] to his favorite haunt known as 'Eagle's Nest' on Eagle Lake, just west of Blue Mountain Lake, to get away from his cups and enjoy the wild life of the woods." And he did indeed enjoy the wildlife, and a wild life.

Buntline visited Piseco on his first Adirondack trip and took over an abandoned hunter's cabin on the Indian River for the winter. In his essay "Burned Out," the writer described his new pure, repentant, back-to-nature existence: "Almost every night I had a concert. A gang of wolves played the principal part. A panther solo made the variations. I was happy. No temptation to deviate from the rules of health and morality appeared. I was at church every day." Paradise was short-lived, though, as the title of the piece indicates: a chimney fire destroyed the little cabin and, along with it, Buntline's desire to play the hermit.

After the fire, Buntline went north and found a cabin and log barn on the shore of an uninhabited lake. (The land had belonged to Gerritt Smith, the abolitionist, since 1836, and the buildings may have been built in the 1840s for free blacks.) Buntline fell in love with the place, known locally as Hog's Nose, and named it Eagle's Nest; he dubbed the lake Eagle Lake.

Chauncey Hathorn, an educated and able woodsman, was Buntline's closest neighbor, philosophical advisor, matchmaker and guide. Hathorn introduced the middle-aged divorcé to Eva Gardiner, an eighteen-year-old barmaid from Troy (or perhaps North Creek), suggesting she'd hire on as a good housekeeper. Buntline, instead of offering her an honest wage, married Gardiner promptly before her first paycheck was due. She died in childbirth within a year of arriving at Eagle's Nest and was scarcely settled underground before Buntline returned to New York for a few months—ostensibly to meet with his publishers, but more likely to find a new wife.

In November 1860 he married Kate Myers, a refined city girl who expected her new home to be a gleaming mansion befitting a world-renowned author, rather than a moss-chinked log cabin miles from the nearest neighbor. In *The Great Rascal*, a biography of Ned Buntline, Jay Monaghan wrote, "Years later, Ned himself liked to tell how he got his bride to Eagle's Nest and then stole her shoes so she could not run away." This marriage, too, was destined to be brief. Despite Buntline's building two new homes, including an almost civilized farmhouse, Myers departed—shoes, baby and all—within eighteen months.

At Eagle's Nest, Buntline entertained congressmen, New York reporters, writer Alfred Billings Street and painter Frederic Church. These noted men, he wrote, "made annual calls when they went to the forest for fresh brain inspiration."

The wilderness provided Buntline with "an ease and freedom I had not known for years." All the while, he was writing serials for the *New York Mercury*, which were featured prominently on the front page of nearly every issue. Although a half-dozen works date from his Adirondack years, there is no whiff of balsam evident in those stories of the high seas and Indian captives. Buntline told friends that when he started a book, he never made corrections or used an eraser. A modern reader paging through, say, *Elfrida, the Red Rover's Daughter* might have guessed that. Buntline wrote, "I once wrote a book of 610 pages in sixty-two hours, but during that time I scarcely ate or slept. As to my method—I never lay out a plot in advance.... First I invent a title, and when I hit on a good one I consider that story about half finished."

Buntline did compose several Adirondack poems, such as "My Maple" and "I Am a Freeman," which was dedicated to the Izaak Walton Club. Ned sent off the verse,

I am a freeman! Tis my boast and pride/The blue sky is o'er me—the dark soil beneath/My bath is the lake—my couch is the heath/My rod and my rifle my larder provide—I am a freeman! 'Tis my boast and pride

which he suggested the club's president could use in the group's newsletter, "or to light a cigar with." Buntline's most popular verse was "My Wild-wood Home," which was printed and reprinted, recited in contests, anthologized, and set to music. A few poignant lines describe Buntline's haven: "Where the world's foul scum can never come/Where friends are so few that all are true—"

Chauncey Hathorn remained a true friend of Buntline's and remarked, "The natives of the country looked upon him as a wonderful man." But local husbands and fathers may not have agreed. Harold Hochschild, author of *Township 34*, a history of Blue Mountain Lake, commented that, "according to repute, Ned's less formal liaisons were spaced never more than a few months apart. Like his serials, before one ended, another had begun."

The Raquette Lake guide Alvah Dunning didn't see Buntline as a wonderful man, either. In the era before hunting laws, Dunning took his deer when, where and how he chose, which didn't sit well with Buntline. The writer shot one of Dunning's trespassing hounds, launching a feud that was the talk of the North Country. Years later, when he was a somewhat more subdued gentleman, Buntline wrote, "As to Alvah Dunning—God help the poor fellow—I would not hurt a grey hair on his head, if there are any hairs left. He used to annoy me, as he had annoyed others, and I quietly let him know that there was a law of self-defense, that ruled even in the wilderness."

Buntline's musings about acceptable behavior notwithstanding, he did choose to lead a lawless and rowdy existence at times. Stories persist that when Buntline periodically visited the nearest post office, in Lake Pleasant, about thirty miles from his home, he celebrated his arrival by going on a hellacious bender. Then he'd need a few days to recover and a few days to provision and a day to get home, so nearly a week was used up in order to send off a manuscript. It's no small wonder then that his publisher hired Prentice Brown, a farmer who lived at Sprague's Clearing, near Indian Lake, to pick up and deliver the mail. Buntline anxiously awaited Brown's visits.

An entry in his Eagle's Nest diary from 1862 reads, "... six o'clock and no Brown—he'll not come to day! And tomorrow most likely he'll go to Cedar River to attend his Sunday school & the Cedar River brats that haven't got any souls to save."

Buntline's public exploits were also duly chronicled by the North Country press. *The North Creek Journal* noted, "The bars of Glens Falls were within reach and he used to ride his little French pony down there decked out fantastically with bright ribbons braided into his long and heavy mane. His caper of riding his pony into a saloon one day and stopping in front of the bar is remembered by many of our older citizens."

During his last season at Eagle's Nest, in 1862, Buntline spent his time halfheartedly farming, cutting and selling enough hay to pay off the property, and growing hops, turnips, potatoes, cucumbers and watermelons, according to his diary. But the farmhouse was too empty for Buntline, and the call to war—the Civil War—was too insistent. A few months after Kate Myers had left with their baby, Buntline joined New York's First Regiment of Mounted Rifles. (Though Buntline attached the title "Colonel" to his name when the Civil War was over, Union army records show that E. Z. C. Judson was honorably discharged as a private.) In *Township 34*, Harold Hochschild wrote, "If Ned failed of distinction on the battlegrounds of the Civil War, he achieved it during the same period in the field of matrimony by living with two wives at the same time."

In 1867 Buntline sold his Adirondack holdings. He was restless, tired of the woodsman's role and in search of new material. He went west, fascinated by the wide open spaces and their poetic potential. Purely by chance, Buntline met William F. Cody, a carpenter, real-estate agent, occasional Indian scout and cowboy, in Nebraska. At the time, neither man had the slightest inkling about what they would eventually do for each other.

Cody cut a dashing figure, and it took Buntline only a few months to build a legend out of the sketchy details of the life of "Buffalo Bill." Stories about the frontiersman became wildly popular in serial and novel form, and it proved to be only a short leap from page fame to stage fame.

In December 1872 Buntline invited Buffalo Bill and Texas Jack (plainsman John Omohundro) to join him in Chicago as stars of a show called "Scouts of the Prairie." The two men arrived in Chicago on the next available train, only to discover that the impresario (Buntline) had failed to hire the requisite Indians and bad guys, and that the playwright (also Buntline) had not yet written the script for the show, which was to premiere in three days. But, displaying grace under pressure, and with the assistance of every hotel employee who could write, Buntline created the original western drama in just four hours. It was a whole new art form, complete with buckaroos, painted warriors, dancing Indian princesses, rope tricks, blazing six-shooters and a token temperance lecture by "Cale Durg" (Buntline again). Audiences in Cincinnati, St. Louis, Rochester, Albany, Boston and beyond loved it, but in New York City the reviews were lukewarm at best. *The New York Herald* wrote: "The representation was attended by torrents of what seemed thoroughly spontaneous applause; ... Hon. William F. Cody, otherwise 'Buffalo Bill,' occasionally called by the refined people of the eastern cities, 'Bison William,' is a good-looking fellow, tall and straight as an arrow, but ridiculous as an actor. Texas Jack is not quite so good-looking, not so tall, not so straight, and not so ridiculous."

Buntline cranked out more tumbleweed thrillers, under an annual contract for $20,000 with the publishers Street and Smith; Buffalo Bill and Texas Jack got royalties plus income from the shows. In 1873, though, the mustachioed cowpokes broke with their creator to choose another official biographer. But this mattered little to Buntline, who had other heroes to mold in Wild Bill Hickok and Wyatt Earp.

In the mid-1870s Buntline married for at least the sixth time and hung up his rifle, chaps and spurs for good, returning to Stamford to live at a country estate he named Eagle's Nest. By 1880, Buntline was able to retire on his royalties. But in his later years, he mined his Adirondack memories for several short pieces that he sold to *Turf, Field and Farm*. These were hunting and fishing yarns with Buntline as the larger-than-life hero; some of the stories closed with remarks on how progress had perverted the Adirondacks he once enjoyed.

"It makes me sick to go there now," he wrote. "A lover of Nature and Nature's gifts shudders at the advance of—dudes and their fancy accessories. Hunters and anglers go beyond civilization if they know themselves." His last sporting essay was published in April 1886, and he died on July 16 of that year, reportedly of heart disease. Buntline's passing was noted in all the newspapers; his funeral was the biggest occasion Stamford had ever seen.

After his death, Buntline's novels mostly gathered dust, his adventures were forgotten, his political beliefs were discredited. By the turn of the century, there were just a handful of his cronies who kept his memory alive. Leon Mead, a friend and fellow writer, remembered, "Ned accomplished more literary work than Walter Scott and Dickens put together." Maybe. In reams of paper and gallons of ink, it's tough to argue with that assessment, but don't try to check out *Mortimer Monk*, the *Hunchback Millionaire*, or *Merciless Ben, the Hair Lifter* from the Great Books section of your local library.

On Verplanck Colvin's map of Blue Mountain Lake there is a rocky squiggle with the legend "Buntline's Island," and part of the Northville–Lake Placid Trail follows what old-timers still call the Buntline Road. A decaying corner of Buntline's log cabin was recently moved from Eagle Lake, to be displayed on the grounds of the Adirondack Museum.

Ned Buntline's young bride Eva Gardiner, their baby and Buntline's chum Chauncey Hathorn all lie under the pines on the Protestant side of the Blue Mountain Cemetery. But other than these few scattered remnants, an occasional tall tale and the mournful howl of coyotes heard across a frozen lake, there's little left in the central Adirondacks that recalls that celebrated scalawag.

—NOVEMBER/DECEMBER 1991

Adirondack Eldorado
There was only fool's gold in them thar hills

FROM THE RIVERBANKS near Sutter's Mill, forty-niners searching for the mother lode described the tract as rugged and empty; cold, wet and buggy was the word coming back from gold seekers in the Klondike. On the face of it, the Adirondacks, New York's blank spot on the map north of Saratoga, had a fair lot in common with those real goldfields. Flowing from the mountains there were braided ribbons of likely looking sandy creeks; the valleys held megatons of glittering pebbles and hundreds of square miles of uninhabited land; the settlements cradled an ample supply of men with more shovels than sense. All the right ingredients were readily available in the North Country, except maybe the requisite basic bedrock geology. That detail didn't really matter to all the dreamers and schemers. As the tidal wave of men flowed west to find gold in California in 1849, and the surge then washed back eastward to the Comstock Lode in Nevada and on to the Black Hills of South Dakota in the 1870s, the Adirondacks inevitably got caught up in the undertow.

On the surface, that ebb and flow might seem an apt image, but in fact the first Adirondack gold claims predate all that

Western mine fever by several generations, harking back to the earliest days of New York State record keeping. In April 1793 a farmer near Whitehall registered the second gold find in the state, along Wood Creek. Within months, most of his neighbors made the trip to the secretary of state's office in Albany to record their claims. They filed on their own lands, on the farms next door, beneath barns across the lane, and underwater; in this state, even today, anyone can claim gold and silver anywhere, regardless of who owns the land.

And lay claim they did. By the late nineteenth century, there were prospectors of both sexes exploring every corner of the Adirondacks. Folks named Emmogen, Amasa, Luther, Amateus, Isaac, Jabez, Abegale, Asa and Quebec George were out with pick and pan, digging weasel holes, pits, trenches and sluiceways. In Fulton and Hamilton Counties, these goldhounds filed thousands of claims with the Register of Gold and Silver Mines; Washington and Warren County streamsides spawned hundreds of would-be mines. People truly believed that there was gold in them thar hills, and in muddy Twitchell Creek; along the South Branch of the Moose River; under the frothy Hudson and Sacandaga Rivers; somewhere on Black Mountain, in Jay; atop Fish Mountain, near Lake Pleasant; in Mason Lake, Whittaker Lake, Mud Lake and Oxbow Lake; beside Kenyontown, Elbow, Dummings, Overrocker and dozens more creeks, named and unnamed; at Paris and Burcalow Springs and even under the county courthouse at Sageville, now Lake Pleasant. It's almost easier to catalog where there weren't any gold claims, but those towns were few. Tupper Lake and Lake Placid seem to have been left out of the scurry; Newcomb had just one claim during the 123 years of official state records.

Gold hunting in the Adirondacks really picked up in 1879, after the Black Hills strike had faded in the public memory. Ansel Scidmore, a businessman from Appleton, Wisconsin, began sifting through the gravel near Newton's Corners, now Speculator, and found enough traces of ore to get enthused, if not agitated. By the next summer, Scidmore, his partners, acquaintances, enemies and persons he never met were making daily pilgrimages to the notary public in Northville to record their claims. Most of the activity by then shifted to the towns of Benson and Hope, which together had more than two hundred entries in the state mine register.

Amongst all these hoary records, which carry the indisputable verisimilitude that accompanies old things, is one belonging to Richard Rosa, dated July 30, 1880, written in an elegant hand on pages of a crumbling leather-bound ledger: "... I hereby give notice that I have discovered a mine of gold and silver in the county of Hamilton.... The metal is found in large lumps free from quartz or other worthless matter. The lumps vary in size from a quarter cup to a bushel basket. Location: The bottom of the central portion of Lake Pleasant in the Town of Lake Pleasant. The lead commences at that point and runs thence perpendicularly until it strikes the upper confines of China."

The *Albany Evening Register*, in December 1882, acknowledged the Adirondack Eldorado, describing mines bearing frontiersy monikers like the Otter Gulch, the Naomi, the Tryon, the Boulder Gulch. Reportedly, the gold found in the gravel near Benson assayed at nearly eight dollars a ton, which was a very profitable margin for the technology of the day. A plant was to be constructed that could process some fifty tons of sand and gravel per day, but apparently things never progressed quite that far.

As the likelier spots in the southern Adirondacks were snapped up on paper and in person, attention shifted to the north. In the 1890s, a Saranac Lake blacksmith named Edward Dobbins blasted a hole fifteen feet deep into the side of Mount Pisgah. His gold paid out at a meager buck fifty a ton; his insistence that burrowing deeper into the mountain would bring great reward only made potential investors even more skeptical. At about the same time, according to a 1930s-vintage newsletter from the Trudeau Institute, an Algonquin Indian from Three Rivers, Quebec, appeared at the sanatorium's lab with ore samples he claimed were from Saranac Lake, which assayed out at the respectable percentage of fifteen dollars a ton. Exactly where this gold came from remains a mystery.

Even the staid and generally reputable *Scientific American* took notice of the Adirondack gold quest in 1898. That year there were some 5,000 claims filed in the state: "... thousands of prospectors are excited by the finds in northern New York, and Hadley, Warren County, seems to be in the center of the territory now creating interest." This gold in the Hudson was stuck to river sand. It proved difficult to separate, so it was pulverized and collected by the "quicksilver process."

As the claims proliferated, the news spread, technology developed and the influx of more educated—and perhaps more shady—outsiders grew, it was inevitable that the promise of Adirondack gold was transformed from the wishful thinking of local farmers to highly engineered swindles by Boston- and New York–based corporations. As dozens of extravagantly titled geologists and eccentric inventors came onto the scene, the notion was spread that the elusive Adirondack gold existed in an "unripe" or "green" state, and could be brought to profitable maturity only through mysterious processes. That was hogwash, of course, but more than one white-coated, wing-tipped wonder ripped off schoolmarms, loggers and hardscrabble settlers.

Franklin County, which had only seventeen claims filed in state mine records, turned out to be the most fertile location for bogus gold ventures. The Riverside Gold Mining and Reduction Company of St. Regis Falls issued a prospectus for stock in 1904 that urged townspeople to take advantage of the golden opportunity to participate in the all-but-certain success of a local concern. With the railroad nearby, and the inexhaustible waterpower of the St. Regis River, the mine was situated in a prime location; it was believed the ore was "nearly limitless." The stock offer suggested that "it is possible that every investor of $25 at present [gold] prices, after three years will be placed in comfortable circumstances for the balance of his life." To add credibility to the project, board members included the local school principal and the state representative from Malone. Ralph Farmer, a local history buff, wrote that "according to the old-timers, the stock sold very well and everyone thought they would be rich. The story goes that two men were sent to buy equipment for the mine and disappeared with the money."

Within a few years, national journals were actively trying to steer people away from putting their money into Adirondack gold. *The Engineering and Mining Journal* reported in 1911 that most North Country gold really assayed at something less than a dime per ton of rock. It also described an oft-repeated scenario: "For some unexplained reason, after the mill is up, the machinery in place and all made ready for operation, the gold does not materialize for the stockholders."

The Black Mountain strike, in 1910, "seized the entire north slope of the Adirondacks in its pulsating grip and shook it out of a long winter's lethargy," wrote Warwick Carpenter, in *Outing*. Supposedly, a vein of gold-bearing quartz was discovered in Jay, with an astonishing purity of $55,000 per ton, but this, too, was proven false.

The most spectacular swindle made the front page of the *New York Sun*; the headlines screamed, "Gold from Sand ... Stock Exchange Members Find They Were Dealing with Ex-Convict and a Wonder Machine." The company, Twentieth Century Gold Extracting, had nearly 2,000 acres in Santa Clara and Waverly, and its stock was traded on the New York exchange. The key to the promised 200 to 600 percent profits was held by an Englishman, Edwin Jordan, who insisted Adirondack gold was "fine grained and very volatile." His research had led him to believe that the reluctant metal could be coaxed out of the air—transmuted, in the alchemist's words—through magnetic pulses and radiation. He told a reporter, "There is no question about there being tremendous quantities of gold here, and we can get them out. I have been studying radium and its action ever since Mrs. Curie discovered it, and when Professor Rutherford by the use of uranium nitrate transmuted copper into lithium, I went deeper into it." Jordan insisted he had no monetary stake in this, that the reward was in the pure scientific application of his revolutionary processes. His palaver worked well enough to separate many Massachusetts businessmen from thousands of dollars; it's unclear how much stock was sold following the exposé.

The Engineering and Mining Journal had the last, best word on the North Country Klondike: "Not all of the Adirondack gold 'miners' are swindlers; some of them are merely stupid.... Our notice to suckers is that Adirondack sand contains only green gold and that green gold is the stuff that gold bricks are made of."

—JANUARY/FEBRUARY 1993

Radical Chicks
Hatching a bird-brained plot

SEED CATALOGS PROMISE so much, but after a while the pictures of voluptuous, pendant fruit just seem so irrelevant to Adirondack gardening. As if watermelons would thrive beyond golf-ball stage in Blue Mountain Lake. Or that you could actually harvest okra in Olmstedville. Besides, who really wants to grow pumpkins so plump you could hollow them out for hot tubs, or livid purple broccoli that turns a weak chartreuse when it's cooked? No, on dreary mud-season nights when I entertain thoughts of spring fantasies, I turn to my favorite poultry catalog. Staring back at me in regal splendor are perfectly matched cockerels and pullets: stately Partridge Wyandottes, in forest green, chestnut, buff and black; Dalmatian-speckled Lakenvelders with perky crimson combs; huge, feather-footed Cochins, like plumage-covered basketballs. Then there are the bantams, from trim, feisty Old English Games to Silkies covered with fine, angora-like down that drapes from topknot to tail, alongside perfect diminutives of the classic birds, such as little Leghorns, Rhode Island Reds and Plymouth Rocks. I skip over the truly bizarre birdlife, the naked-necked Turkens, the Easter-egg layers and the Polish fowl, which look like ordinary chickens from the shoulders down, but above are ruffed, muffed and fluffed into something particularly silly-looking, escapees from a Dr. Seuss book.

Mail-order chickens—what a concept. Available in every rainbow shade, harking from every corner of the world, and the post office will deliver them in a bright, peeping box after winter's end but before the onset of summer.

My husband and I came to be Adirondack poultry fanciers through the back door, thanks to a former landlord who left us a surprise gift of six bantams, three scrawny roosters and three tired hens. The bantams turned out to be charming. The roosters could fly like pheasants and would roost high in the trees, the better to serenade the neighbors when dawn was imminent, or at least less than four hours away. The hens scratched for bugs, chased bees and dashed around the yard. Sadly, even though one hen set all summer long on what appeared to be several dozen eggs, chicks were never in the picture. We were hooked though, and it was only a matter of time before we expanded the flock.

I had seen classified ads in the papers offering chicks with strange-sounding names like Sex-Links and Golden Comets, but I wanted something more old-fashioned. A catalog from faraway Iowa showed page after page of chromolithographs of chickens; the pictures looked like formal portraits, downright nineteenth-centuryish, but the technology for raising the birds was thoroughly modern. And of course they'd deliver to Blue Mountain Lake; they'd ship after March 1.

We went crazy reading florid poultry prose and studying the attributes of the various breeds. No sense in getting high-strung Mediterranean chickens for this climate; their wattles would get frostbite in the winter. Although the idea of a home-grown chicken barbecue seemed sort of amusing, turning lots of birds into meat items wasn't our plan. So we settled on the company's brown-egg-layer assortment, which promised dozens of comfy, prolific hens, plus a few exotics like an infant Blue Andalusian rooster. If he turned out to be the henhouse bully, we thought, not only would he make a dandy cacciatore, but we could also make trout flies from his hackles. We dispatched the order and built a brooder out of an old coffee crate.

Nothing on earth is so astonishingly prompt as the U. S. Mail when a boxful of chicks is in its custody. It seemed like mere hours had passed between the time our order was confirmed and our postmaster called. "Hurry," she said.

I think now that that unusual alacrity could only have been caused by one thing. Not concern for the welfare of the tiny creatures, nor an aversion to the faint farmy smell coming from beasts in a box. It was the noise, only the noise. The sound of one chick peeping is kind of appealing, but the racket of fifty of them shrieking for their lives could constitute a punishment most cruel and unusual.

That first batch of chicks grew, thrived, scratched in the yard, ate countless blackflies, laid large eggs that were more coveted than the season's first ripe tomato and provided hours of entertainment. Those birds were followed by others from that Iowa hatchery—pinstriped Barred Rocks, tall Brahmas, no-nonsense New Hampshires.

These days we're not in the poultry business, since our new house is on the edge of a woods populated by bears, coyotes and foxes, but every spring we think, *hmmm*, maybe it's time once again to fill the yard with darting, squawking, brightly colored birds. Perhaps we'll go for a monochromatic look this time, with a palomino flock of Buff Orpingtons or a dozen glossy black Langshans, and maybe get a few lavender-gray guinea hens, just for the excitement.

—MARCH/APRIL 1993

Straight Shooter
Katherine Elizabeth McClellan was the North Country's first camerawoman

I make a point of composition. It is absolutely essential to good photography, and while to the artist form and color are equally important factors, to the photographer form is everything. Color, as such, only appeals to him as gradations of light and shade.... First of all, then, the form and subject matter of your picture should be picturesque in outline; it should have balance, symmetry, a foreground, middle distance and distance, each having suitable relation to the other, according to the impression you wish to convey. There should be one point of interest and one only, and it should be placed somewhat to the middle of your picture. Correct composition will be clear, direct and restful to the eye." — Saranac Lake photographer Katherine Elizabeth McClellan, interviewed in an 1899 issue of Wilson's Photographic Magazine.

THE ADIRONDACKS AT the turn of the century provided professional photographers with an unlimited wealth of visual material and a growing clientele eager for vivid images of memorable places. The acknowledged leader of the cameramen was Seneca Ray Stoddard, whose innumerable views, stereographs, lantern slides, guidebooks and maps made him rich and famous throughout the Northeast. There were plenty of other professionals operating in and around the Adirondacks, including G. W. Baldwin, who had studios in Plattsburgh and, later, in Saranac Lake; H. M. Beach, who was based in Tug Hill and ranged as far as Star Lake, Chazy, Lake Placid, Inlet and Blue Mountain Lake, capturing images of downtowns and resorts; J. F. Holley, a chronicler of small-town life, in Chestertown; and Alonzo Mix, from Warrensburg, who specialized in farm scenes and local portraits. The outsider in this group, in more ways than one, was a thirty-something single woman named Katherine Elizabeth McClellan, who, beginning about 1893, pursued a successful career as a photographer of artfully conceived Adirondack landscapes. Not content with merely recording the scenery, she placed models—a woman with a parasol, a man leaning against a fence—within the frame to create a painterly vision, and she arranged for solo exhibitions in major cities that would bring her views to art critics and new, appreciative audiences.

McClellan was born in New Jersey in 1859, and graduated with the first class at Smith College in 1882. She worked as a school principal, an instructor of Latin and English and a private tutor before moving to the Adirondacks with her father, who was a physician, her mother and her sister, Daisietta, a tuberculosis patient who came for treatment at the Adirondack Cottage Sanatorium. Dr. McClellan was named Saranac Lake's first public-health officer, and he also developed its first exclusive planned neighborhood, Highland Park.

With her father's initial backing, Katherine McClellan quickly built up a business in an area that then had no full-time, resident professional photographer. She sold prints of mountain and lake scenes, and produced souvenir books for the tourist trade, including *John Brown, or A Hero's Grave in the Adirondacks* (1896) and *Keene Valley* (1898), which were filled with quaint images and descriptive prose. The Lotus Press, in New York, printed *Keene Valley*. (Although it sounds like an art-book house, the company's backlist included family histories, amateur poetry and publications for fraternal organizations—it was, in other words, a vanity press.)

The John Brown book sold for a quarter; the paperbound *Keene Valley* book was fifty cents. Both were available by mail order for an additional twenty-five-cent charge. McClellan wrote the text: "Keene Valley! The very name calls up memories of the most delightful drives along the river road; up and over the hills where new vistas of mountain peak and valley meadow are constantly revealed; of trips by boat through the loveliest of Adirondack waters; of climbs following trails to the tops of the giants which encircle the valley ..." The slim, sage-green volume contained useful information, too, on the Adirondack Mountain Reserve, the Adirondack Trail Improvement Society, the Keene Valley library and suggestions on lodgings and guides.

McClellan also published calendars with scenes from Bloomingdale, the Saranac lakes and Lake Placid. This was a new approach: even Stoddard hadn't yet designed calendars as a vehicle for marketing his pictures. Her photographs appeared in the 1896 *New York State Forest, Fish and Game Report* and in *An Adirondack Romance*, a popular ladies' page-turner. She began work on souvenir books for Saranac Lake and Lake Placid, although it appears these were never completed. In 1900 she opened a summer studio at the Hotel Champlain, on Bluff Point, where she advertised the availability of "artistic studio portraiture, and out-of-door poses, miniatures, and tinted photographs." The hotel provided a base of operations for expeditions to Ausable Chasm and to Champlain Valley towns for more salable views and a captive market for her images.

In 1898 the Pontiac Club Carnival edition of the *Adirondack Enterprise* published a glowing profile of McClellan. "Her collection today embraces most of the finest views to be found in the region. A carriage ride each summer through a hitherto unexplored locality adds new pictures to an already extensive collection, and the long winter months are spent in preparing them for the market which is always a ready and profitable one ... One of Miss McClellan's landscapes selected from among hundreds of equal worth, is a source of satisfaction and inspiration forever."

Following solo exhibitions in New York and Philadelphia, McClellan received the critical acclaim that she sought beyond her Saranac fans. *The New York Herald* described her works displayed at a swank Fifth Avenue gallery as "high art photographs.... In a region abounding in wild beauty, Miss McClellan has selected its most picturesque spots. Among the most interesting—there is rarely one that is not worth studying—are those of Ausable Chasm, Wilmington Notch Falls, John Brown's Grave, A Storm Effect, etc." *The Philadelphia Public Ledger* commented, "Miss McClellan shows herself master of a very difficult art, and combines a fine sense of the artistic with that knowledge of a practical character which contributes so much to the success of a photograph."

It's unclear how McClellan learned her craft; no beloved teacher emerges and there are no records of camera-club memberships, workshops or apprenticeships. Although hundreds of her images survive, only scattered documents persist that provide a glimpse of her life away from the viewfinder. (In the 1890s an increasing number of women were avidly pursuing photography as a hobby, as an artistic outlet and as a career. Technological advances in cameras and other equipment made the venture more accessible. Mass-produced dry-plate negatives and factory-sensitized papers greatly simplified darkroom processes; improved view cameras held magazines with a dozen or more negatives, so that multiple shots could be taken without reloading. By 1900 more than three thousand female professional photographers were counted across the country, but women who specialized in landscape photography were a very small minority indeed.)

In an 1899 article in *Wilson's Photographic Magazine*, Camera Club secretary Richard Hines highlighted leading women photographers. (His was among the first such articles in a national journal.) Hines's shortlist of the best and the brightest included Catharine Weed Ward, an Albany native who took up photography in 1886 (Ward was a highly regarded lecturer, magazine and book editor, and photographer; her book, *Shakespeare's Town and Times*, was deemed a masterpiece. When she left her post at *American Amateur Photographer*, she was succeeded by

Alfred Stieglitz); Mathilde Weil, from Philadelphia (Weil was primarily a studio photographer whose works were displayed alongside those of the leading male photographers in critically acclaimed national salons); and Katherine McClellan, the only woman Hines discussed who worked primarily in outdoor settings with natural light.

McClellan outlined her start in the business in Saranac Lake to Hines: "After a year of varying successes and failures, my father built me a small studio—a one-room affair—which seemed a very paradise, but by another season, two more rooms were added, and this season [1898] I have just finished a two-story building." She described her winter exhibitions in New York and Philadelphia as very successful.

In 1903 McClellan left Saranac Lake to photograph the Connecticut River Valley. Shortly thereafter she became the official photographer for Smith College, where Henry James, Harriet Beecher Stowe and other prominent figures of the time sat for their portraits in McClellan's studio. She was profiled in *Good Housekeeping* and *New Idea Woman's Magazine*, and her works were prominently displayed at the Panama-Pacific Exposition, in San Francisco. In 1916 McClellan and her sister moved to Sarasota, Florida—then a small country town—where they developed an exclusive subdivision complete with paved sidewalks, streetlights and a private yacht basin. McClellan continued to take pictures, traveling to Nassau, to Seminole Indian homes and to rural Florida farms and communities. She volunteered at an aviation-training camp as World War I was coming to a close, managing a kitchen that fed several hundred servicemen every day.

During the 1920s she returned to the Adirondacks to tend to some business deals in her late father's Highland Park development, and in 1922 built a summer home in Saranac Lake, named the Kath-E-Mac Camp, that she enjoyed for more than a decade. She continued to oversee building in Highland Park, according to Smith College alumnae notes. Her last Adirondack scenes refer back to her first: views of the John Brown Farm.

Katherine Elizabeth McClellan died in September 1934. Her glass-plate negatives and prints are preserved at Smith College

Archives and Historic Northampton, both in Northampton, Massachusetts; Clinton County Historical Society, in Plattsburgh; and the Adirondack Collection, at the Saranac Lake Free Library.

—JULY/AUGUST 1993

Sorry, Long Number
Hung up on the party line

WHILE I WAS away in late April, a few things happened in Blue Mountain Lake: the ice went out, a new postal officer was appointed, and through the wonders of modern technology, every household was launched into the digital revolution. Some more willingly than others.

As long as most people I know can remember, and right up till the spring of 1994, our town was its own little island of communications simplicity. We could call anybody around here by using just four numbers. That used to be the case elsewhere in the Adirondacks into the late seventies, but Blue Mountain was the last to hold on to its own version of speed dialing.

As you might expect, it was easy to memorize lots of phone numbers, and so it wasn't any big deal to help somebody who had called a wrong number. Here's an example, loosely transcribed from a call at 6:45 one morning (with names and numbers changed so as not to embarrass anyone): "Lambert?!" "No, you want 9922." "Oh, right. Sorry." "No problem, Mike."

Most of the time, local wrong-number calls—to my house, anyway—ended up being people I didn't mind talking to, just to catch up on town affairs.

The four-number club made us feel a bit special; one small

aspect of twentieth-century life remained uncomplicated. It was so simple in fact that many preschool-age kids were quite skilled at making calls to family and friends. I remember one such conversation in which a very young man rang me up to give me important gardening advice. "Betsy," he said, "this is Danny. You should go out with your jackknife and cut the suckers off your tomato plants." "Right now?" I asked. "Yes," he said gravely. To this day, I'm not sure what surprised me more—that he called me all on his own or that he was right, my tomatoes were in need of serious attention.

The four-number deal was made possible by antiquated equipment, which admittedly had its occasional downside. Calls to Long Lake, a mere ten miles away as the moose meanders, sounded at best like talking via tin cans and twine, and at worst like a shortwave-radio transmission from Vladivostok. Waiting for a long-distance call to go through seemed to take a longish while. It was generally just enough time for me to pour a cup of coffee, add milk and sugar, stir, take a swig, and have the other person pick up to catch me gasping and sputtering, trying to swallow in time to say hello.

Now what we have are "custom-calling features" for "pennies a day!" according to an upbeat newsletter from our local phone company. (Which, I must add, announced it was selling most of its access lines in New York to a major utility company that operates gas, electric and water lines, along with wastewater treatment plants. My imagination has run wild with interesting scenarios involving potential disasters, repairmen, billing errors and so forth, but I'll hold back here.)

The list of these services includes "speed calling," described as "great for senior citizens and young children!" But we already had speed calling, and it worked fine, thank you. Now we can opt for "call forwarding," so that people can follow us around rather than wait until we're home again. And we can try "three-way calling," so that we can talk to two people in two different places concurrently. This is touted as something that will help with "planning family gatherings" (clearly, the phone company's copywriter is an only child) and "committee work." I remain skeptical. Conversations involving three or more people in a small town are meant to happen outside the post office or over a cup of coffee in a diner so that there are witnesses and others who can relay the information to other potentially interested parties.

What I really dread, though, is having my first Blue Mountain Lake encounter with "call waiting." I can imagine listening intently to some amazing tale of woe, or chattering away recounting my own fascinating saga, only to be cut off mid-sentence by that irritating *click click* as the person on the other end says, "Gosh, can you hold on a sec while I check this other call?" Especially when I know what he or she really means is, "Wait right there, inconsequential neighbor, while I deliberate your relative worth. This other person is most likely far more important than you." Call me old-fashioned, but I always thought that a busy signal was a pretty clear indication that a) someone was home where you were calling, b) they were already talking on the phone and c) if you really wanted to speak to them, you could try again later.

So far, the technological triumph of cellular phones has yet to penetrate Blue Mountain. The signals get tangled up in the tamaracks, swallowed by porcupines or carried away on the wings of blackflies. Progress is inevitable, though, and I'm sure I'll someday see somebody on top of a wild peak with portable phone in hand, yapping away to some office-bound person lightyears away.

I'm preparing a secret weapon for that future shock. He's a very large, gentle, silent dog who loves to snatch things like hats and mittens from people. I think by the time the cellular revolution comes, he'll know just what to do.

Ready, boy? Reach out and touch someone! Good dog!

—JULY/AUGUST 1994

Why We Bagged It
Keeping shop till we dropped

WE MOVED TO the Adirondacks in March 1976 and became gradually cemented in place by the accumulation of certain worldly goods: woodstove, chain saw, snowshoes, canoe. Collecting experiences helped us put down roots as well. We learned how to make maple syrup (don't tap cherry trees, for starters), how to execute a proper do-si-do, how to swim in frigid waters (the first lesson coming after sinking a friend's sailboat because we forgot to check the drain plugs, and the second after demonstrating white-water canoe strokes without informing our dog what we planned to do). We joined the fire department and the ambulance squad. But nothing was quite so declarative of our notions to become part of the community as going into business in downtown Blue Mountain Lake.

It was spring 1980, and my partner and I were both on unemployment following the end of the Olympics and the demise of CETA. Once a week we had gone to a church basement in Tupper Lake to correctly answer the Three Big Questions: Were you able to work? Did you look for work? Did you refuse any work?

Next!

Clearly there was no future in that activity, and few full-time jobs loomed on the horizon. There was a tantalizing prospect, though, since the old general store in town was for sale at a reasonable price. We attempted to buy the place, but someone else moved more quickly. They desired the property as an investment and had no intention of running a business, so we ended up as tenants.

Our strongest asset was ignorant enthusiasm.

What could be so difficult about running a grocery store? Why, we had spent countless hours buying and eating food! Our combined experience in retail sales had been limited to part-time jobs at a ski shop and a discount department store, which didn't exactly prepare us for being owners, managers, cashiers, butchers and bookkeepers, but we had ideas about the possibilities of being merchants.

We had about six weeks to get the place washed, painted, refurbished and stocked. We had to find suppliers for groceries, produce, meat, soda, beer, dairy products, ice cream, newspapers, candy, crackers, chips, bread, ice, bags and sundries; it turned out there were two or three companies we had to buy from in each category, because, for example, Coke doesn't sell Pepsi. The bills began to pile up, what with orders and repairs to things like compressors for walk-in coolers. Then there were permits to get, paperwork to file and deposits to pay.

We connected with a huge wholesaler for our main grocery supply, and the Syracuse office sent a salesman to walk us through our first order, which was utterly mind-boggling: imagine every item you could possibly expect to find in a compact but well-stocked grocery store, then order a couple cases of it. Then think of all the things you don't like and would never in a zillion years waste your money on, and order some of those too.

Then pay for it all. Because we were new customers, our first order—thousands of dollars' worth of ketchup, toothpicks, dish soap, onions, soup, baby food, dog biscuits, paper towels, TV dinners—was cash. Not a check or money order, but actual dollar bills exchanged for a tractor-trailer load of stuff. The salesman helped us arrange the shelves according to the protocol that dictates the olives go next to pickles go next to vinegar and so forth. Within hours, the place looked like we were in business, and we had totally blown years of savings. Even if we failed miserably and no one came to our store, we wouldn't starve, we rationalized, and if necessary, we'd learn to make wholesome meals out of condiments.

We opened on May 15, offering free coffee and cookies. Folks came, drank coffee, said nice things and left. We got some good advice—"Eat your mistakes at home," "Don't let anybody talk you into charge accounts," "Take orders over the phone, but don't do it for free"—and hired a couple of strong, tireless teenagers and a savvy neighbor so that the store could be open seventy hours a week. My partner and I took Sunday afternoons off, but that was all.

The building itself was what drew us into commerce. A solid, three-story structure, for more than half a century it had anchored the community, providing all the necessities and more than a few luxuries. A small room had served as the post office for several years, and the upstairs, a vast open space about thirty by sixty feet, once sold hardware and dry goods. The nail bins were still there along the wall and a wire rack for lantern chimneys hung above a display table. Under the eaves were the records for M. Callahan and Company, boxes of bills with ornate engraved letterheads and the odd, charming mementos of town life from long ago: a poster for the House of David basketball team playing in North Creek and miniature slates for ordering staples like blacking, bluing, codfish, currants, sago, sal soda and saleratus. The place hinted at a tradition that we hoped we might recapture, and perhaps even profit from.

We got to know our suppliers, who provided a human link to that past. As you'd expect, they were older men, independent guys who worked long hours. There was Milton, who went to the Syracuse farm market at four a.m. each day, then drove north to sell produce to restaurants, lodges, camps and stores. He marveled when we bought watercress and sold it out in a day. "You've got the trade here," he said, and proceeded to educate us by bringing up ambrosial white peaches, succulent yellow cherries and tiny salt potatoes. There was John, who'd arrive with his dual-axle truck brimming with plump old-fashioned tomatoes he grew on his farm, and Freddy, who was a pirate at heart but always made deals on lightly bruised bananas, slightly limp spinach and other bargains. Ralph the iceman was a gentle soul who refinished barroom shuffleboard rigs and transported them to tournaments in a cut-off school bus during cold weather; he timed his deliveries to our place so he'd arrive just as we were closing up and we could sit in the back office next to the roll-top desk, sipping root beer and listening to him talk of selling block ice from a horse-drawn wagon throughout Black River Valley towns.

The meat purveyors weren't a link with the past but a feeble connection to the future. Our main supplier, in Utica, was in the throes of computerizing its operations, which meant unfathomable bills, mixed-up orders and deliveries that invariably came between midnight and dawn. There's nothing quite as rude as being awakened from a sound slumber to unload cold, dripping boxes of beef, pork and chicken.

Our first big weekend was Memorial Day. It was exhilarating to ring up orders and help customers depart with bulging brown bags. Everything seemed to work; nobody seemed to notice that we were clueless. June was slow, but it offered a chance to practice making hamburger, trimming lettuce and keeping track of inventory.

All hell broke loose in July. Our customers wanted things (rolling papers, condoms, racy magazines) that we never dreamed of selling, and sometimes bought far more off the shelves than what we had anticipated. I spent a sleepless night before Independence Day wondering where I'd find a case of butter to go with the thirty dozen ears of corn we had to sell. My partner gallantly turned huge ungainly hunks of meat into symmetrical roasts and chops (we ate the wedge-shape nubbins that defied categorization). I vowed we'd never run out of toilet paper or disposable diapers. We became snack-food connoisseurs.

We learned a lot about provisions, planning and human behavior. Since most of our daily customers were on vacation, we were witness to subtle social dynamics. For example, no one grocery shops for fun. People have certain expectations of how food stores should work and tend not to be open-minded when things are a little bit different. Dads shop while on vacation, but from our sample it seems that they do not participate much in the activity during the rest of the year. We base our finding on the oft-repeated episode of the man of the house ordering a custom-cut steak the size of Delaware and responding with hysterical disbelief to the cost.

Some people also clearly leave their good manners at home. I spent twenty minutes sobbing in the meat locker after a customer called me a bad name because I had ordered caraway-rye bread rather than dill. Another customer threw lamb chops at my partner, shrieking they were spoiled. (She was wrong. They were delicious.) A frail-looking, determined woman wrenched the lock out of our door when she forced her way in to get a Sunday *New York Times*; apparently she missed the large poster that said CLOSED and couldn't hear us yelling, "Wait! Stop!!"

The newspapers truly were our worst nightmare. We likened summer folks' need for news of the outside world to an addictive drug that blinded them to their immediate environment. On brilliant sunny mornings, when any right-thinking individual would be hiking or canoeing or at least enjoying the fresh air from an Adirondack chair, people would line up outside to get a paper, watching through the window with pathetic hope etched on their faces as we bustled to assemble hundreds of papers from all the different sections. There was a newsprint shortage that summer, so we never quite got our requested allotment. Papers were highly sought after and occasionally caused ugly incidents, such as the infamous *New York Times* tug-of-war.

One summer morning, a female visitor muttered that the twenty-five-cent profit we eked out of a six-pound Sunday paper was despicable and accused us of ripping her off. "Don't buy it," said my partner, gently removing it from her hands. "But I want it," she said, as she yanked back. "Then pay for it," he said, holding firmly on to his end of the bundle. "You're impossible," she shouted as she tried to wrest the paper from his grasp. "So are you, lady!" he said. The other customers cheered as she exited.

That day marked a subtle yet profound change in our attitude. No more tears in the cooler, no more apologies for ground

round that cost two bucks a pound. We realized most of our customers didn't want to have a relationship with us, they just wanted to buy things and get out of the store. We began to understand what our neighbors had probably known all along, that no matter how much we wanted it to, the store couldn't sustain us through the winter. The days when the place was the life-support system of town were long gone. We couldn't compete with the bright lights of Long Lake and Indian Lake, and folks had become habituated to going ten miles down the road to the bank, the hairdresser, the lumberyard, and, yes, the supermart.

We put a last, best effort into stocking the store for big-game season with the kinds of things we imagined hunters would crave after a long day in the woods: hot dogs, Canadian bacon, pork rinds, doughnuts. We were about twenty years too late, though, since most hunters had long ago gotten in the habit of picking up the essentials before they left home. Business dwindled to a trickle, then stopped altogether, which was a good thing because it was awfully hard to keep the building from freezing with one lonely kerosene heater. On November 1, we gave it up for good.

What we gained from those frenzied weeks was all the wieners the hunters eschewed (two full cases, or close to 500; to this day, the sight of a hot dog fills me with a curious mixture of nostalgia and loathing), several cases of cheap beer and soda, lots of canned goods (butter beans, creamed corn and sardines), boxes of Jell-O in assorted perky colors, jars of generic jam, crates of industrial-strength paper products and enough breakfast cereal to last a year. We made about as much money as we would have had we both found minimum-wage jobs. Beyond that, though, the store was an education, a graduate semester in small-townology with a minor in microeconomics. We're not in business anymore, but once in a while we imagine what it might be like to stand again behind the counter on a sultry evening, washed in the wan neon glow of a Genesee sign and counting out change.

—SEPTEMBER/OCTOBER 1994

Wild Life Refuge
The Adirondacks still provides splendid isolation

YOU WON'T FIND *Adam Peverleigh* by Mrs. C. F. Gerry on the shelves of your community library or through the magic of amazon.com. You won't see the 1864 novelette listed in the volumes of the *Adirondack Bibliography* either. I was able to read (make that lurch through until I could lurch no longer) the romance thanks to a friend who's a passionate, devoted collector of Adirondackana. There it was on some dusty shelf, so he bought it.

That *Adam Peverleigh, or The Living Mystery of the Adirondacks* remains largely lost to the treasure halls of regional literature is no great loss at all; the story's full of hackneyed descriptions, absurd cases of mistaken identity and overwrought dialogue ("Hark ye! I will make a dashing reconnaissance, and capture her, if I chance to find her wandering," cries the antagonist, to which his trusted valet responds, "Bravo! Bravo!"). The setting is so faint that it's clear the author was never within a hundred leagues of the Adirondacks. However, *Adam Peverleigh* does introduce some themes that continue to color our mythology: this is a place of both dismal exile and safe haven.

Back in the shadowy stretches of our civilization, wilderness conceptually served as a sinister sanctuary for outlaws, the disgraced and depraved. Only in modern times, since the middle of the nineteenth century, has society put a positive spin on the unkempt edges of the world. But the folks who make their lives in these places seem to remember an ancient debt to those cast away. Maybe it's that life here is hard, there's no need to make it harder on people who arrive by choice or by chance.

Practically every Adirondack hamlet has or had its token "remittance man," the ne'er-do-well scion of a wealthy family sent away to stay out of trouble—or at least stay out of the newspapers. Most settlements tolerated a fallen woman or two, along with smugglers, grifters, artful dodgers and two-bit gangsters. Many towns harbored the scandal-prone, the accused, the acquitted. Blue Mountain Lake billeted just such a scoundrel in Ned Buntline; despite his checkered past, he was never run out of town, and the mail was even delivered to his remote cabin yard. Notorious bootlegger Dutch Schultz was made a Hamilton County sheriff's deputy.

Skim a local paper and you might find passing reference to resident Reds, secret agents, suspected treasoners and refugees of obscure origin. Napoleon Bonaparte's humiliated compatriots fled across an ocean to put down roots in this part of the world, and Benedict Arnold will always be a hero in the North Country.

There's a kind of code of the frontier at work, that acceptance can be won by recent deeds, not a person's past, and that respect may be earned by treating people accordingly. The payback is a small measure of protection against curious outsiders. In places where we know each other's shoe sizes, the ranks close in, depending on the questioner.

Consider, for example, Albert Einstein. Grainy photos from the thirties and forties show the physicist sailing on Lower Saranac Lake; now, we learn, his companion at camp in 1944 was quite likely Margarita Konenkova, reputedly a Russian spy. Throughout his visit, Einstein enjoyed the shelter of his friends and the studied indifference of the surrounding community. Though the local papers noted his presence, the cultured woman with the exotic accent was never mentioned.

Then there's Nixon in Tupper. I can't prove it: my source is long gone, and the feigned confusion of folks who might know for sure only makes me wonder all the more. For argument's sake, I'll take the bait; it's not like there aren't legions of loyal Republicans here who wouldn't gladly give the commander in chief the key to the Chris-Craft. The story goes that following his resignation, Richard M. Nixon spent halcyon weeks on Tupper Lake, cloaked in luxurious seclusion. I had hoped to find his name in the country-club guestbook or hear about his stop at the Sky Line drive-in, but his collaborators remain steadfastly mum.

Which brings us to the recluse of the season, Monica Lewinsky. I can't respond to that sorry saga, but I do salute her alleged choice for refuge. Our North Country is about as far from the seat of political power as an American can get without crossing the border. I'd come here in a heartbeat if I didn't want wing-tipped wonders tracking me down.

I heard that Ms. Lewinsky was hanging out at a grand old camp, one with windows that don't reflect much more than the surrounding pines and a phone in the name of a long-dead ancestor. I heard that she went on boat rides and drank coffee on the screen porch. I heard that she had the kind of low-profile Adirondack vacation that any old twenty-something might have had. I also heard that when the Plattsburgh television station heard the same tales I had, the trail was cold, cold, cold. True to tradition, not a solitary soul was available for comment.

—NOVEMBER/DECEMBER 1998

Taking Stock
A look at the big picture from a small place

BLUE MOUNTAIN LAKE is a small place, to be sure, but it's never a ghost town even on the longest nights of the year. For some reason, though, the question of how Blue Mountaineers spend the cold months is endlessly fascinating to folks from away. They picture us as brave souls battling the elements, living some kind of Laura Ingalls Wilder Little House on the Tundra existence.

"What do you do all winter?" is so common a summer query that it cries out for flippant replies like, "When we're not chewing our husbands' moccasins to keep them soft and pliable, we work in giant igloos with central heat, electric lights and indoor plumbing." Of course no one I know has ever uttered those words—or anything remotely as ill-mannered—but the temptation does arise. Rest assured, concerned visitors, we are not deprived.

When the snowbanks tower and the lake ice bellows like a banshee, we do all the things that ordinary people do—work, play, take care of families, look out for neighbors, enjoy the company of friends, shovel roofs, play snowshoe softball, fight chimney fires, ski, skate, sled, watch TV, cook, clean, feed the birds. On those evenings when we know it's going to be thirty or forty below, the calls are made and the cards come out for night baseball, seven/twenty-seven, spit in the ocean and a raft of other penny-ante games. The night's last bet, though, is whose thermometer will hit absolute bottom. Because our house is the lowest of the bunch, altitudinally speaking, our mercury never scores the dubious honor.

Another tradition of sorts is the annual New Year's census. The first town tally happened about twenty years ago when we were having dinner with friends and someone wondered aloud about just how many people were truly year-rounders. Numbers were tossed around—a hundred, 150—then the challenge was made: "Let's just count everybody." So we did.

Starting at the top of the hill, across from the dump, we began listing people house by house: Emery, Gert, Mary, Lovel … you get the idea. Practically everyone at that gathering was a volunteer fire person, so together we knew the roads with eerie precision and had a pretty solid inkling of who was really home stoking the woodstove and not basking on some Florida beach. The names of townfolk spilled out faster and faster—infants, toddlers, teens, bachelors, newlyweds, widows, patriarchs and great-great aunts, plenty with Irish or French surnames—but the mini-tide of humanity (the figure that year was 138, I think) swept me into a reverie of picturing all these snug little dwellings with neatly plowed driveways, smoke curling from the chimneys and golden light from the windows spilling onto billows of perfect snow. I got lost in a Norman Rockwell scene in which even the beagle houses had Adirondack-green shutters with pine-tree cutouts—timeless, charming and utterly imaginary. Hearing those names spoken with familiarity—fondness, even—made our town appear fleetingly like a tight little island floating in a sea of uncertainty.

At one time I thought I would be a demographer. I would spend my career tracking great waves of migration and measuring population mega-trends. That night I went home amazed that I lived in such a miniature community and that the place was compact enough that it could be counted casually and accurately, as easy as packing fifty pennies into paper tubes. Enumerating everyone in town by a simple roll call should be impossible in modern times.

The New Year's census continues, still offhand, still in the spirit of fun. But each time we tick off gains and losses, I have to wonder if these subtle increments lead us away from noticing bigger changes in the works. In half a century, Blue Mountain Lake has become less self-sufficient (no school, no barbershop, no cows), and old fields have grown into forests, but it remains a handful of roads with a few dozen homes, many of which a long-gone resident would recognize. The name still accurately defines the town, and we're lucky. Every Adirondack settlement has the potential to preserve its honest, imperfect individuality, same as every place is vulnerable to a pervasive virus to become just like anywhere else, without distinctive character or a sense of community. And there are agents of change all around.

—JANUARY/FEBRUARY 1999

A Clue in Clay
An eighteenth-century artifact comes to light

NEW YORK TERRITORY, early summer, sometime in the 1750s: After starting out from Sir William Johnson's lands on the Mohawk River—a four-day trip on foot through thick, damp forest—a party of three rangers stops to camp for the night. Thus far they've bushwhacked along a succession of south-flowing streams; they had heard from a trader that a flat-topped, stand-alone mountain with a lake at its base marks where waters head north. The ground is soft, thanks to days of intermittent downpour, and the bugs are insatiable, thanks also to the rain.

After preparing a simple camp and feasting on partridge (again! and tasting all the world like roast turpentine due to the fool hens' diet of tamarack and spruce buds), one man pulls out his clay pipe to cap the end of a long day. He finds a twist of tobacco that miraculously escaped complete saturation. Somewhere on the long, wet march through the wilds he's lost his brass pipe tamper, so he has to use his thumb to fill the bowl. He fumbles, his fingers damp and numb, and the thimble-size receptacle breaks.

On the other side of the campfire, a companion takes another swig of rum and mockingly launches into a bit of verse, "Little tub of mighty power / charmer of an idle hour / object of my hot desire / lip of wax and eye of fire ... "

Versions of that poem first appeared in England in 1735; the clay fragment emerged from my Blue Mountain Lake garden in May 1999. Tilling this plot always yields springtime surprises—1940s bottle caps, rusty toys, parsnips somehow ignored the fall before now the size and texture of pulp logs—but an eighteenth-century artifact warrants scrutiny.

In eastern Essex County or around Saratoga, such a scrap would be interesting, but not remarkable. For generations, people in those places have been plowing up ancient buttons, belt buckles, even cannonballs. But northern Hamilton County's another story, and one that typically begins around the time of the Civil War.

Naturally, I dug a little deeper. Checked out every bit of debris. Found a minute grayish bit with a raised edge (bone from a large animal, not porcelain as I thought) and a good-size piece of handsome English transferware. The pipe was just too enigmatic to ignore. So I phoned David Starbuck, an archaeology professor who lives in Chestertown and who has led many digs at Rogers Island, Fort William Henry and elsewhere on the edges of the Adirondacks.

His advice was to take a drill bit to determine the size of the bore, which is one way to date a pipe. To summarize reams of research into one cursory statement, a larger stem-hole diameter means an older pipe. This item accommodates a $6/64$-inch bit, putting its manufacture between 1680 and 1750. With that news, I took pipe in hand and went to his house.

Clay pipes made in England and Scotland were ubiquitous and cheap, and as Ivor Noel Hume's *Artifacts of Colonial America* makes clear, the "kaolin tobacco pipe is possibly the most valuable clue yet available to the student of historical sites, for it is an item that was manufactured, imported, smoked, and thrown away all within a matter of a year or two."

So there it was, evidence of an earlier time that local histories have overlooked. Most records—written or remembered—for my town leap from the meltwater of the last glacier to Verplanck Colvin's 1873 visit, when the surveyor found one inhabitant living in a bark shanty.

Starbuck and I discussed the clean-slate nature of eighteenth-century central Adirondacks. The whole place was stunningly absent from the discussions of New York, not even an object of curiosity. Maps of the time portray Lake George and Lake Champlain with eerie clarity, and dismiss millions of interior acres with sketchy legends like "This country by Reason of Mountains, Swamps and drowned Land is impassable and uninhabited." To our minds, it's likely that traders and scouts passed through parts of the region on foot or by dugout canoe. They would have known about temporary Indian camps on waterways like the Rock River and Long Lake and sought native contact for furs and information about troop movements, fortifications and routes.

Testing local lore is a dangerous thing; new material isn't always welcome. Some scholars, I'm sure, will argue that my clue in broken clay fell out of somebody's pocket in the 1890s, when the land I own was cleared. But how likely is that?

—JULY/AUGUST 1999

Notes from a Small Place
When local color fades away

IN 1969, THE YEAR ADIRONDACK LIFE magazine began, there were more than 11,000 people living in the Adirondack Park who had been born in the nineteenth century. Now all but a handful are gone, and with them has disappeared a history that was as real—and ephemeral—as the tang of chewing spruce gum or the jingle of workhorse harness. When I moved to the central Adirondacks in the mid-seventies, it seemed that practically everyone I met had honest-to-goodness pioneer memories.

One neighbor had been born in a lumber camp somewhere east of Blue Mountain; even with good directions and a GPS unit you'd have a tough time today locating any artifacts that proved nearly two dozen people lived there—ate, slept, sang after dinner and played cards within four walls that must have reeked of damp wool, sweat and fried pork.

As a boy this neighbor earned money setting pins in the bowling alley at the nearby Prospect House, a technological marvel, the first hotel in the world to have an electric light in every room. In antiques shops you can sometimes find a picture of the place, with ladies in long white dresses standing statuesque on the veranda; and there, just down my street, was someone with firsthand knowledge of the hotel, the Irish girls who worked in the kitchen, the stockbroker guests from Manhattan, the stagecoach driver and steamboat pilot who brought them all to Blue Mountain Lake. It seemed remarkable that a living person should be carrying these relics around in his brain.

Another friend worked on Hudson River log drives and knew every bend that caused jams and every sweeper-turned-keeper where some nonswimming 'jack had stepped off a slippery log and into eternity. He could explain why there's a cross carved high in a pine towering over the river between Newcomb and the Black Hole, remembering the gray face of the dead man and his wide staring eyes. The first time I walked through the forest with him, it was like he was Adam, naming the wild things for the first time. He called a pileated woodpecker "cock o' the woods" and dug up some woodland delicacy he dubbed "trinkle root."

Another acquaintance, daughter of a guide and Great Camp caretaker, met William West Durant as a passenger on the *Tuscarora*, the steamboat that went from Marion River Carry to the lodges on Blue Mountain Lake. When the boat passed the Prospect House, she recalled Durant looking ruefully at its massive white bulk, shaking his head as he muttered, "Now that was a mistake." She told how her father stood up to his boss, who owned a vast place west of Raquette Lake. He had suggested the caretaker let a fire get out of control one winter so that a new, improved camp could be built; the deed was done. When that same man had forgotten to pay her father hundreds of dollars in back wages, the caretaker said it would be a terrible shame if the "old red horse came galloping over the mountains again" and took down the new palace. Within days the back pay appeared.

A few bars of "Auld Lang Syne" here. Bear in mind, though, some say that title translates into "old long sins." Murder, arson, poaching, blackmail, crimes, misdemeanors and accidents—not everyday life—percolate to the peak of a person's memory. But it's also the ordinary vignettes that nail things down, stories of going to a dance by bobsleigh in the next town, and no, it didn't matter a bit when the man at the reins fell asleep on the way home that night. The horses knew the way, and all but removed their own bridles when they reached the barn.

When I was new in town, the stories were prolific. It was as if information on bygone ways was linked to a person's DNA, which all braided together to form a community. In the old days, and fading fast by the 1970s, towns eleven or twelve miles apart were as distinct from one another as different kinds of apples. Now they're blurred, blended like supermarket cider. Common threads aren't families so much, trades or even affiliations, but items like Grand Union groceries, franchise minimarts, chain discount stores, big things from away.

When the magazine began, virtually all Adirondack business was local. Towns had barbers, undertakers, gas stations, diners, firmly woven into the domestic fabric. Owned in town; operated in town; taking cash in, dispensing wages out, all in town. If you went to the bank for a loan, it was approved not just for the way you filled out the application, but because you were a known quantity, someone with a past—and if you got the loan, a future. In twenty-three years I've watched our nearby bank go through five different corporate names, each incarnation successively more out of touch with local needs. Today, at this bank and its branches, you can't make a loan payment at the counter (mail it, friend) or exchange Canadian cash for greenbacks.

The list goes on. Pharmacies used to be independent affairs; the druggist was as knowledgeable of your family as was the general practitioner who prescribed the medicine in the first place. Now drugstores across the Adirondacks (with some notable exceptions) are tendrils of national franchises, leaves on some exotic vine, offering comfortable sameness, consistent pricing and identical layouts. Luckily, many pharmacists still operate in the old ways, despite corporate overlays; they counsel older patients, arrange for delivery to shut-ins and perform other services not in their job descriptions.

Then there's food. Adirondack fast food in 1969 was a cup of coffee and a doughnut in a diner at ten in the morning, after every other breakfaster had gone but considerably before the early lunch crowd arrived. Now Burger King, Pizza Hut and McDonald's perch along the roadsides, conveniently spaced so no town is farther than thirty miles from the closest fast food. Depending on your point of view, these shiny boxes add either a numbing sameness to a stretch of generic highway frontage or a reassuringly familiar facade and the promise of clean restrooms.

The Adirondack economy of the old days has been likened to a colonial economy, with resource extraction as the core. Pay was low; finished products were made somewhere down the line, as were the decisions about harvesting what, where, when and by whom. We may be even closer to a colonial economy today, as franchises replace mom-and-pop businesses one by one.

So what's the good news about the last thirty years? For one thing, our standard of living is better. There are more year-round jobs, thanks in part to government agencies. Roads are better; more are paved, and snow removal is state-of-the-art. Medical care keeps up with technological changes. There's public radio now, better TV reception, improved telephone service. The cultural scene is far livelier. A mere handful of arts groups were around in 1969, struggling to build audiences and stay afloat. Today there are scores of organizations, from resident professional theater and musical groups to dance troupes, historic-preservation groups, music festivals and advocacy councils. There are more libraries today than there were thirty years ago, in towns (Long Lake and North Creek, among others) where citizens took it upon themselves to build these institutions from scratch.

And there's more there out there. More miles of navigable waterways, more acres of wilderness, more wild forest, more primitive land that belongs to all of us.

—COLLECTORS ISSUE 1999

A Noble Set
Following in the bootsteps of a wild bunch

IF THE ADIRONDACK guide didn't exist as a living, breathing action hero we would have invented him anyway. Every distinctive landscape has some kind of rugged, romanticized historical figure that arose from a particular way of life: the cowboys of the Great Plains, the voyageurs of the upper Midwest, California forty-niners, Maine lobstermen. Guides are a bit different, though, in that the profession was a response to how other people chose to experience wilderness; for the first time, outdoor recreation—not a commodity like beef or fur or gold—was fueling a local economy.

When settlers first moved to the Adirondacks from New England and Canada, they came to farm, cut timber and mine ore. Sometimes they scraped a living together performing all three, so adding another cold-cash task to an already complicated resumé wasn't that big a leap. Likewise adding a room or two onto the family farmstead for out-of-town guests who wished for a real bed before they opted for balsam boughs in a bark shanty was a logical step too. By the time America had recovered enough from the Civil War to appreciate clean air, wild country and the pursuit of happiness as embodied by fish and game, the guides were there to show people the way. For two bucks a day—a bargain even then—you could hire a man, his guideboat and a couple of rangy hounds to create your own adventure.

All this hardscrabble independence, though, set up a service caste that had no intention of ever being servants. As photographer and guidebook author Seneca Ray Stoddard saw it, "they are, as a class, a noble set of men who see themselves as the equals of their employer." Truth be told, after a long day pulling at the oars followed by setting up camp, preparing dinner and all but tucking the exhausted sports in for the night, I suspect many woodsmen felt a tad superior to their clients.

Guides came in all shapes and sizes, from "tall, bony, shaggy, one-legged" Chris Crandall, who took Ansel Judd Northrup around Meacham Lake and secured immortality through the pages of *Camps and Tramps in the Adirondacks*, to corpulent Ed Arnold, from the Fulton Chain, remembered now for his skill with a fly rod and timber-rattling snores. Typical guides were idolized with assessments like S. H. Hammond's "as jolly, good-natured people ... albeit rough and unpolished" standard issue in the popular press. Old Mountain Phelps charmed the urbanites with his fluffy beard, archaic outlook and peculiar figures of speech, delivering, according to one writer, "his sage conclusions and whimsical oddities in cheery, chirripy, squeaky sort of tone—an octave above the ordinary voice, somewhat suggestive of an ancient chickadee."

Some observers, though, saw the flaws as clearly as the flash. In the 1870s Stoddard met up with Raquette Lake guide Alvah Dunning and reported, "Old Alvah was in his normal condition—suffering from ill treatment. He has always been a sufferer.... " North Elba's Bill Nye was recorded as "silent, morose even"; other guides, we may assume, with underwhelming personalities and middling woodcraft skills, faded back into the woods.

The larger-than-life legacy of the old-time guides leaves us with a beloved cast of colorful characters, more than a few trails up the High Peaks and an altered ark of native beasts. If it's true that Mitchell Sabattis killed nine panthers and twenty moose during his decades-long career, his modest demeanor was not a charade for the benefit of outsiders. There were far more productive hunters, like John Cheney, who bludgeoned a wolf to death to save his own skin, and who tallied 600 deer, 400 fishers, thirty otters, six wolves and possibly the last beaver left in the state. The champion bipedal predator may have been Elijah Simonds, who claimed he killed "three thousand foxes, two thousand deer, 150 bears, twelve moose and seven panthers, besides more mink, otter and martin than any other man who lived in the Adirondacks," according to Charles Brumley in *Guides of the Adirondacks*.

Luckily, the guides themselves realized their excesses were taking a toll. Some of them urged the state to create hunting, fishing and trapping seasons as well as bag limits. Market hunting, which had provided meat for many hotels, was banned; dynamiting fish, hounding deer and night hunting were all outlawed by the early 1900s.

In the twenty-first century, the Adirondack guide's job description has changed. He or she may be called upon for rock-climbing, wild-food gathering, bird-watching or instruction using a global positioning system as often as to lead a sport on the trail of a white-tailed buck. And the guide's clientele has changed too, from mostly men in the prime of life to children, women or senior citizens—which is a good thing, since we all could benefit from the experts as we learn the ways of the woods.

—SEPTEMBER/OCTOBER 2000

Percy's Back Pages
A great American writer's private life in Saranac Lake

"As if a magic word had been pronounced, the assorted streaks, the formless blobs of white, the crisscross of ribs, coalesced and sprang out in a figure of perfect beauty and perfect meaning. He looked into the very depths of a being, a being as translucent and complex as some undersea creature, a crystalline space closed about by upcurving ribs. The heart stood out in the round—he could have taken it in both hands. At each side the great vessels, as gnarled and convolved as roots, were joined by the bronchi, hollow striped tubes, to branch out twining into the lacy substance of the lung in a complex arboresque of which he could see every twist and turn.

He was reassured: it could not be too bad—the structure was too beautiful."

THE WRITER HAD active tuberculosis, as you might guess from his comments on reviewing his X-ray, but I had to travel far beyond the Blue Line to read that observation in a folder of typewritten pages at the manuscripts collection of the University of North Carolina. The excerpt comes from an unpublished novel set in Saranac Lake, *The Gramercy Winner* by Walker Percy (1916–1990). If you're not familiar with his work, here's a start: Percy's first novel, *The Moviegoer*, won the National Book Award in 1962. *Love in the Ruins*, published in 1971, an apocalyptic tale about a race war somewhere in future America, cinched Percy's reputation.

Percy was a true Southern writer, with all the intensity and intellectual baggage that entails. Yet there it is in downtown Chapel Hill, a rare thing to a student of regional letters: an Adirondack book about real life by one of the great American authors. Write what you know, urge countless literature instructors, and Percy knew TB first-hand. It changed his life, making him a writer rather than a doctor.

Percy graduated from medical school in 1941, and during his first year as an intern contracted the disease not from a patient but from a tissue sample in the pathology lab. He went to Saranac Lake just as America became fully involved in World War II, but turned his thoughtful attention to town life rather than outside events. "What a strange place—where thousands of sick people, and yet somehow not really sick, lay abed month after month on deep verandahs, tucked in, silent, still, watchful, as the seasons came and went, where thousands got well and stayed on, bewitched by the old mountain village."

The story follows the path of William Grey, a recent Princeton graduate, who arrives in Saranac Lake after just one week in the Marines; a lesion on his lungs has rendered him unfit for service and bound for the san. He ends up in a cure-cottage attic, hoping for a bed in the "Adirondack Lodge," a lovely green campus modeled after Trudeau Sanatorium. Some of his housemates have been there eight years—waiting, lying in bed for hours and hours, submitting to treatment that included collapsing lungs with a long hollow needle, spitting into disposable cups. For several older patients the cottage is "no way station, but home," a place they would leave only when they died.

For a couple of years Walker Percy watched, learned and wrote about the transformative nature of illness, the hard truths to be addressed despite the surrounding aura of home and help. "In a life where all was made easy, where everything conspired for the comfort and cheer of the patient, there came ever so often these times of reckoning when the grim nature of the struggle could no longer be concealed. If ordinarily the way here was made a thousand times easier than life outside, then there must inexorably come these periods of judgments that were a thousand times sterner; when, despite all the good will and graciousness of doctors, nurses and kin, the question which had to be put and answered was nothing less than: am I getting better or am I dying of it?"

I read the book in one sitting, taking notes, thinking about the connections with real places and real people, imagining how folks in Saranac Lake might react to statements like "A strange thing happens to a man when he comes up here.... He feels a peculiar license—it is the opposite of the juridical process: he receives his sentence first, that is, he gets his tuberculosis, and he reserves himself the privilege of crime later. This is a strange little place, Willy, not subject to the laws and levies of the United States. Haven't you heard, for example, that the marriage contract is invalid north of Utica?"

I wish I could announce the imminent publication of a significant book of regional interest, but attempts to convince Percy's literary executor of the novel's value to a North Country audience have been met with polite refusal. The prognosis for *The Gramercy Winner* is to stay where it is, like a lab specimen of some forgotten ailment, available for scholars to read and dissect under the watchful eye of an archivist.

—NOVEMBER/DECEMBER 2001

Leaving Church
Adirondack Life *says goodbye to its longtime home*

EIGHTEEN THIRTY-EIGHT: the foundation is dug, the bricks have arrived by oxcart from across the river, the wagons packed with straw and panes of bull's-eye glass from Redford are expected any minute. The committee, after consulting books, magazines and far-flung relatives from larger towns, has decided to build a church in the Federal style, a bit behind the times, but then fashion has always been slow to arrive in the North Country. In the builders' minds this structure would be austere yet welcoming, substantial but not ostentatious—something to last for generations.

And so it stands today, across from the village green in Jay, historically preserved but fulfilling a function far from its original mission of serving a community's spiritual needs. Funerals, weddings, baptisms and suppers were all part of the brick church's year.

There must have been tearful sessions during the Civil War, heartbreaking memorials in World War I, a host of tragedies that rocked this town, now only footnotes to local lore. Throughout the events of a harsh outside world, the congregation soldiered on.

There may have been politics from the pulpit too, as local Liberty Party leaders Jesse Tobey and Pierrepont Jones brought their abolitionist message to this corner of the world. Being a member of the Liberty Party in the 1840s was as radical and strange as being a member of the Green Party is today.

The place is a window on the past, even during the days of ADIRONDACK LIFE's tenure here, from 1987 to 2001.

From an upstairs vantage point on Earth Day 1990, we watched in befuddlement as the stand of beautiful cedar trees in the park was felled to make way for a new flagpole, a new gazebo and a new fountain. I guess the town fathers preferred the village green to be more grass than grove. We also looked over the smoldering ruins of McDonald's General Store. Kitty-corner from the church, it was an anchor of the community in an entirely different way—former post office, feed store, deli and a place to get a six-pack for those late nights putting the book together. We also saw the demise of Hurley & Madden's store, next door, where buffalo-check shirts could be had for ten bucks, or a soda or an Aladdin lamp wick. That store, we learned, was the setting of James Thurber's short story "Josephine Has Her Day." The literary light was already shining here when ADIRONDACK LIFE arrived on the scene.

The church had its highlights, acquiring a flush toilet well before the Baptists down the street got theirs, and low spots, such as the downfall of Vincent C. Moore, bank officer, church leader, pillar of the community and—what he will be remembered for instead—embezzler. Mr. Moore, it turns out, was the toastmaster for the brick church's centennial celebration as he was quietly stealing the hard-earned money of his friends and neighbors. In 1938, anticipating that he would be found out, he headed to Au Sable Forks, drank lye and died.

The church has had its share of wildlife inhabitants, from pigeons and bats in the belfry to skunks in the strip of trees at the back of the building. We never cozied up to the pigeons, but one bat, Lumpy, flitted around the sanctuary for a day until we figured out a humane way to send him outdoors. The skunks were civilized neighbors, hunting for grubs in the leaves in the morning and venturing out to the lawn by late afternoon, the three kits trundling together from point to point like a rugby scrum, shoulder to shoulder.

The building was divided upstairs and downstairs, with the business and advertising offices on the ground floor where the kitchen and dining room once had been, and the editorial and production staff in the sanctuary, a soaring, airy space where ideas floated like Nerf footballs (along with some actual Nerf footballs from time to time). Ad production was on the third floor but the choir loft was only used for storage.

I say "was" because as you read this, ADIRONDACK LIFE will have left the sanctuary behind, heading up the road to the former Paleface ski center. We need more space and Paleface should meet our purposes well.

We move on, but memories remain. On September 11 the peace of the sanctuary offered small solace to the handful of us huddled around our computers, trying to make sense of the day. And on September 12 we hung a flag from a second-floor window—one that had flown from the *Arizona* memorial in Pearl Harbor—connecting us, the church in downtown Jay, with the larger world.

—JANUARY/FEBRUARY 2002

Waste Watching
Pondering trash as the tie that binds

THE HAND-LETTERED SIGN that appeared this summer in the Blue Mountain Lake post office contained all the information a person would need about the local landfill, but the words "All Are Welcome" stopped me in my tracks. Not that I've ever felt unwelcome at the dump—these places don't discriminate—but I wondered if I ought to bring a covered dish to pass the next time I arrive with a truckload of brush.

Twenty-first-century Adirondack dumps are arguably the most egalitarian facilities in the park, where rich and poor, posh resort and backwoods camp share the bins, boxes, sheds and bucket loaders. Landfills are public spaces for disposal of our private lives, where last week's edition of *National Enquirer* snuggles up to *Barron's*, and gallon jugs of Royal Host tawny port glint next to the dusty shoulders of Opus One.

Landfills have long been centers for the efficient, anonymous, moneyless redistribution of goods. Amid the hillocks of household debris can be found not-so-busted furniture, not-so-worn-out appliances and even antiques. I once rescued a captivating lithographed-tin contraption for testing batteries, with slots for the C and D cells. It spun around on a star-shape base and was topped with an embossed chrome star and a miniature bulb that lit up when a battery was placed in a cradle. I envisioned the artifact as a table lamp or, at the very least, a gift for some suburban relative with a house known for tasteful things.

Anthropologists have written reams about the village refuse heaps of third-world countries as valuable levelers of entrenched class differences. I read this in a college text, only to find myself benefiting from the unencumbering gifts of remodeling summer residents: huge wooden drawers from an outmoded kitchen and heavy-duty hardware from doors now defunct. Mention dump-picking in a polite gathering and raised eyebrows outnumber approving nods two to one. There could be a politically correct phrase for the pastime, like secondary shopping or free-market, free-will merchandise transmission. Our full-service transfer station has a trailer for items too useful to discard, with a placard saying "Always Wal-Mart" in Magic Marker scrawl.

Dumps once were entertainment, with flocks of buzzards gracefully wheeling against a cobalt sky and families of bears performing for appreciative audiences. We used to think that grabbing out-of-towners, getting some ice cream and standing on the edge of a stinking cliff on a summer twilight was a fine evening out. As darkness descended, creatures emerged from backstage. A chorus of raccoons trilled in the wings as bears—stars of the show—went through their routines.

When local landfills closed in the nineties—most have been replaced by cargo containers that are trucked to central megadumps—town boards actually debated the potential loss of tourism dollars and discussed creating food stations for wildlife. That ill-advised scheme would have lacked the weird voyeurism of seeing noble creatures debasing themselves by consuming our own disgusting detritus.

Accumulations of rubbish made the leap from individual to collective only in recent times. Our farmhouse, modest in acreage and everything else, is prolific in its piles of ancient trash. I've found more than a half-dozen dumplets, most out of sight from the kitchen door yet a quick walk away. Trees have grown atop heaps of intact whiskey bottles and the carcasses of tin cans, testament to the staying power of certain materials as well as the tenacity of hardwood saplings. Of course, recycling wasn't an issue then: food scraps went to the family dog, pig or chickens. Containers, like flour sacks or lard buckets, had intrinsic value. Things were used to the last atom.

Modern transportation arrived at about the same time as packaging designed to attract the consumer as much as protect the contents. Farming declined, and communities found a new service was necessary: space away from homes for garbage. Some public dumps evolved organically; one old Blue Mountain Lake byway turned into the heave-ho highway when a new state road was built. Along this slice through the woods are big defunct things, from sewing machines to wagon wheel rims.

North Country landfills are surprisingly antiseptic these days. Construction-and-demolition debris has its own corner, the mounds of bricks and boards shadows of the dumps of yore. Glass and metal get sent far away, sometimes finding willing buyers, sometimes getting buried. Garbage itself is entombed in plastic bags, which can last for a decade before breaking down. Toss in some Styrofoam cups—bound to keep their molecular structure for thousands of years—and you're left with a real legacy. Just as I prowl through my woodland stashes looking for information about the people who lived here before me, we give future folks plenty to ponder.

—SEPTEMBER/OCTOBER 2002

They Shoot Trees, Don't They?
Time will tell if timber theft laws take root

SOME PEOPLE COUNT sheep to fall asleep; I count trees. I picture walking around our land, noticing the knobs punctuating a beech trunk, the lightning-shocked top of a seven-foot-diameter hemlock that appears alive and well at head height. I check the gradual decline of a leaning swamp maple and scan the broom-bristle-thick tamaracks. On our twelve acres there must be a thousand trees, occupying a typical mixed northern forest, a wet-footed swale, grown-over pasture and almost a sugar bush. Biodiversity? It's here, in green, brown, gray and gold.

Of course, this isn't only my woods. It belongs to me, my husband, our dogs, a queenly doe and her fawns, a gray fox, a rabble of raccoons, a squadron of flying squirrels, a jury of turkeys, partridges, woodcocks, red-eyed vireos, bats, moths, efts, toads, peepers, creepers and all the rest. We don't manage this place so much as keep track of it. The dates when lady's slippers and interrupted ferns emerge are as noteworthy as the amount of BTUs a certain nearly deceased yellow birch may yield.

We haven't posted this property and don't much mind sharing the unremarkable wildness with passers-through. We're not aware, generally, of others who walk in and out unless we see tracks in fresh snow or a bootprint in the sneaky grass-covered gumbo that masquerades as solid ground. For hunters, the place isn't all that productive. It's also a bit close to civilization, or at least the kind of civilization practiced on this dead-end lane, population two. One November morning I looked past our garage and spotted a hunter squatting next to a big cherry tree. He may have considered himself well disguised, but he was in plain view to me. I yelled to offer him a cup of coffee, breaking his eagle-eye concentration, spooking the game—which hadn't been around since deer season started. Bucks in some parts of the Adirondacks keep fairly accurate calendars.

A hunter on watch is one thing. The snarl of a chain saw is another. That sound anywhere within earshot warrants speedy investigation. It riles us in the same indignant way that enormous out-of-state SUVs do when they fly down the county road at double the speed limit. That act, however, if caught, gets you a ticket and a massive fine. Steal someone's sawlogs, and you may settle the matter with spare change.

Back in 1909 New York State set penalties for taking trees off public or private land without permission. Today, a rustler may pay as little as ten bucks per tree. The fine is absurd; a veneer-quality cherry or sugar maple can be worth three grand off the stump.

Lest this seem like an archaic issue, stealing timber remains big business. Near Huletts Landing a couple of years ago an unscrupulous logger drifted off one woodlot onto another, clearcutting thirty-one acres of fine hardwoods. The landowner discovered the denuded landscape, and the culprit was apprehended.

Despite blatant examples like that, not much enforcement goes on. A forest industry insider explained that state police don't take the crime seriously and are concerned more with catching the person who took your TV than the one who cut, skidded, loaded and hauled away lumber when you weren't watching. Pursuing tree poachers often falls to Department of Environmental Conservation officers and forest rangers, but the misdeed gets little attention in local courts.

For seven years, laws intended to fix this situation have withered in Albany like so many drought-stricken saplings. Timber theft legislation earns appreciative nods from environmental groups and backing from the forest industry. It never takes root. The latest version, State Senate bill 5574, sponsored by Senator Ronald Stafford, passed that house last spring. The Assembly has yet to consider bill 9190, the same legislation, despite the urging of the Attorney General and the governor. In the new law, timber theft would earn a $250 fine and be treated as a Class A misdemeanor. (Other crimes in that category include petty larceny, menacing and unauthorized use of a computer.) If there is a lame-duck session this fall, and whether the Assembly discusses the proposed law, is anyone's guess.

Part of the push to pass this bill this year comes from the Adirondack senator's retirement in December. Without the protective "Stafford Shield," the process starts over next session, shepherded by less-senior sponsors. They may lack the power Stafford accumulated from years on the finance committee, and the bill would languish again.

One North Country custom I've been curious about is shooting your Christmas tree. I know about firing a shotgun at apple trees as a fast way to prune them, but I've been told that skilled marksmen can decapitate a tall balsam with one slug. It's not just stumps that prove trees have been stolen, but topless conifers too.

—NOVEMBER/DECEMBER 2002

Scorched Earth
Arson in the Adirondacks: a hot topic for two centuries

SEDUCTIVE, DESTRUCTIVE, ROMANTIC, terrifying—fire fascinates and transforms, especially in the Adirondacks. The starlit night in the lean-to by the lake is made whole by a crackling campfire; the archetypal rustic retreat includes a fireplace as the centerpiece. Hearth equals home.

Even the forest we see today, an endless carpet of combustible material, is that way because of blazes large and small, going back long before man hit the scene. Dig a hole and you'll find ancient ashes. Look over a beautiful white-birch ridge and understand that species moves in after the ground has been disturbed by flames. Close to a million acres burned in a five-year span at the beginning of the twentieth century, leaving behind a new landscape populated by new insects, birds, mammals, flowers, shrubs, trees.

Fire has been society's constant companion since the region was settled in the eighteenth century. Champlain Valley towns, struggling to civilize hostile territory, fell to the flames of invading armies, first the French, then the British. The soldier's most effective tool in creating widespread terror was not a musket but a torch. How could an isolated farmer defend his home and barn against a simple pitch-rich chunk of burning pine tossed into a haystack? How could a thrown-together town of frame buildings keep sparks from leaping roof to roof in a typical North Country breeze? Arson shaped the earliest settlement patterns, obliterating communities until peace reigned. And arson remains a basic tool in removing surplus property, threatening rivals, exacting revenge, making a political statement.

In the 1880s Adirondack guides saw the little lake steamboats as direct competitors for their clientele, who had been content to travel at an oar's pace cramped in the stern seat. The new boats, some accommodating dozens of passengers, offered comfort and speed. Waterways were altered to make passage possible. A few new dams were blown up by disgruntled guides hoping to secure the status quo of water levels and their livelihoods. Some commercial steamers disappeared in mysterious ways, slipping beneath dark waves with their hulls stove in, but the demise of Lake Placid's *Mattie* was a spectacular conflagration. Persons unknown set her ablaze at her mooring one night. Their actions only slowed the progress of mass transit a little bit, and within a generation, guides, lake steamers, even the log or clapboard hotels they visited, were memories.

Igniting the rambling old inns that had outlived their usefulness in the age of automobiles was so common that fires were noted, rarely investigated. "Adirondack lightning" occasionally resulted in a check from an insurance company; more often it merely created a convenient clearing for some other structure. Cranberry Lake once had nineteen hotels ringing its shore, and not a vintage one remains. Many burned. Accidents or deliberate acts? A kerosene lamp or creosote-clogged chimney could spawn accidental fires—or the carelessness could be calculated.

"A certain resident of Indian Lake who had twice collected insurance on fires in his store," wrote Harold Hochschild in *Township 34*, "announced one day that he had to leave the next morning for Glens Falls on business. On the dawn of his departure he pulled down the window shades, packed his personal belongings into a carpetbag, planted a lighted candle in a pile of wood shavings on the floor and left the building, locking the door behind him. On his arrival in Glens Falls late that night, he found awaiting him a telegram from his neighbors reading: 'Come back, we put it out.'"

The property owner as arsonist is one thing, almost understandable, except for putting firefighters at risk and ripping off insurance underwriters. Arson comes in many forms, carried out by thrill seekers, pyromaniacs, aimless youngsters, spiteful ex-employees, gung-ho firemen wanting to be first on the scene, even those trying to make an ethical, political or philosophical point about the people behind the structures. During the late twentieth century, some Adirondack fires have defied the profilers, remaining unsolved.

The rambling, abandoned buildings of the Lake Placid Club came under repeated attack by match and gasoline. A dozen fires, destroying five buildings, occurred between 1991 and 1996, keeping Lake Placid police and firefighters as well as Essex County Emergency Services staff busy. Some historic structures were obliterated; other blazes set on porches weren't much more than distractions from more serious work. Alcohol, Tobacco and Firearms agents and an FBI arson expert were enlisted in the inquiry. Suspects were interviewed, and a man was chased down the street late one fiery night. No arrests were made, however. (Two eighteen-year-olds were charged with accidentally starting a fire on club property involving a golf cart, a lighter and some fumes. In the process of checking the cart for gas in order to steal it, a shed burned. But this turned out to be unrelated to the other blazes.)

On or about May 29, 2000, a remote camp on the 50,000-acre Adirondack League Club tract near Old Forge disappeared, leaving only charred sticks behind. Then another went up in smoke in June 2001. And another, around May 1, 2003. Two weeks later, a replacement for the first wrecked place was smoldering history. The fires were perplexing, since the structures were far from any public road. A person would have to hike miles, go past locked gates. A person would have to know the camps were there. The places had no electricity, so faulty wiring couldn't be a factor. Lightning hadn't occurred. Some wonder if spring—and high water levels on the South Branch of the Moose River—may have improved access to these buildings. (The river, open now to white-water paddlers, was the backdrop for a multimillion-dollar lawsuit against the Sierra Club that was settled in June 2000.) The investigation continues, bolstered by a $10,000 reward offered by the club. Will these backcountry homes be safe from matches or monkey-wrenching this spring, in light of stepped-up scrutiny?

—MAY/JUNE 2004

If These Walls Could Talk
Deciphering the history of a house

MOST OF US buy used houses. A used house, though, is not like a pre-owned car. With an automobile, you lift the hood, check the tire tread, go for a test drive. When you acquire a structure, there's more ambiguity and usually no warranty period while you learn its quirks and charms.

Sure, you can ask the seller about energy efficiency and carpenter ants. You can poke and prod the attic insulation and crawl in the crawl space. You can bring a marble and let it roll across the kitchen floor. But until you deconstruct the building, literally or figuratively, you don't know it.

Our home has a cellar with huge boulders laid up nicely. I can stand up in it, but almost no one else can. They risk banging their foreheads on the floor joists, springy hemlock saplings with bark still clinging. This space marks the original house, two rooms downstairs about ten by twelve each, with two similar rooms above. A steep stairway smack in the middle linked them. Viewed with your back to the sunset, the shape is a tall thin rectangle topped by a triangle, exactly the house a first-grader would draw, with skinny windows one atop the other. The space was tiny, but probably quite warm; the old upstairs floors show where two stovepipes came up from the early kitchen and parlor. This section was likely built in 1880 or 1890, from materials found nearby, like those hemlocks and glacially rounded rocks.

About twenty years later, when children and a little more cash entered their lives, the residents added four more rooms, two up and two down, with a handsome quarried stone foundation. Again, they used poles to support the floors, which were made of wide spruce boards from a local sawmill and caulked with sticky, fibrous oakum. Picture another modest house, sketched by a fourth-grader, with a shallower roof pitch, stuck at a right angle to the first one. This addition necessitated a different stairway, one hugging the east wall. It also needed more heat, so another woodstove or a kitchen wood-burner was installed downstairs. This ell is bigger than the first bay, south facing, and a long porch was built to make an inviting public facade.

When my husband and I bought the place, twenty years ago, it was covered in red clapboards, the paint as corrugated as crocodile skin from years of sun. The roof was white—an odd shade for asphalt shingles, we thought. That touch was the bright notion of people who, paying about 8,000 bucks for a couple of acres and more than a few headaches, brought the house back from a wreck in the mid-1970s. Uninhabited then, it had four feet of water in the basement (alligators down there, crocs on the walls). They did some things right, like drying the subterranean lair, but latexing the roof was a big mistake. The shingles shrank and curled, the rain dripped in.

The roofs concealed two other problems: chimneys suspended inside upstairs closets. Since they had been chopped off when the roof was replaced we had little idea they were there. Other tenants had removed downstairs walls that had supported the weight of the bricks, and slowly we noticed sagging ceilings in our dining and living rooms. Sure, you can roll that marble to check for droopy floors, but a ceiling is deceptive. Only when it's like looking up at a pregnant whale belly is the situation obvious.

The bedrooms were interesting. One, big enough for a double mattress and dresser, also contained secret chimney number one. In front of that cell was the cluster-fly hospice, with huge windows perfect for the insects' last days. Across a small hallway was an utterly unusable twelve-by-twelve-foot cubicle, primarily appreciated by cats, long-gone and numerous. Secret chimney two was here. We did not feel like we were violating historic artifacts when we attacked the masonry. It was filthy work, clouds of soot cascading down with the crumbling bricks. But as soon as the offending weight was gone the downstairs ceilings began to rebound. We knew the house had some built-in give, like a ship, but this reaction was a marvel to behold. In the rear of the house was the nicest bedroom, with windows on three sides and big enough to swing the proverbial feline.

Though many facts emerged as we undid so-called remuddling, it's not clear when actual plumbing appeared inside the walls. It could have been as late as the 1930s, when the family took in boarders. We know this in a roundabout way: tearing out the linoleum upstairs, we found pages from a Baltimore newspaper and letters addressed to a professor somebody, care of the homeowners. He apparently stayed for a month or two each summer during the Depression, hanging out at an Adirondack farmstead. He could have seen Blue Mountain Lake from the back door, or by strolling the pasture. Today enormous balsams and soft maples have crowded the view. Hog fencing and barbed wire running smack into tree trunks prove this was a real farm.

By the 1950s working the land was a dim memory here. The barn, just north of the house, was knocked down, a small garage put up. A new kitchen—with Sears cabinets and a gas stove—came next, plus an upstairs bathroom with all modern conveniences, including a window barely above the tub, offering anyone in the driveway a wonderful impression of the bather. Beneath this addition with yet another roof pitch came a real cement-block basement, about fourteen feet square to hold a gas heater and chipmunks. The story of this unremarkable house and its many iterations unraveled as we renovated, taking out a wall here, a floor there, a window and door over there. We had no photos to guide us as we imagined the place a century or even sixty years back. We had the hard evidence: cut floorboards, strange framing and those nasty chimneys.

When we bought it we simply knew it felt like home. The

interior spaces were bright and airy, not claustrophobic. The clapboards gave continuity, and the windows and doors lined up. The variety of foundations wasn't apparent until we stopped to think about what they meant, how the stones and sticks told the story of a poor family putting up a farmstead, enlarging it as more kids and even strangers came along. We're now part of the puzzle, attaching our own porch and downstairs bedroom where the woodshed was. How four walls and one roof became a complex polygon with four distinct peaks and two gabled windows is something we comprehend, but to the next owner the place may seem as organic and seamlessly whole as the clump of white birch trees in the front yard.

—COLLECTORS ISSUE 2005

School's Out

For the first time in 105 years Raquette Lake has no school

IN SEPTEMBER seven Raquette Lake kids will be waiting for the bus, anticipating the first day of school like thousands of others across the Adirondacks. This fall is different, though, because the bus won't stop at the local school, on Route 28, but will continue fourteen miles down the road to Blue Mountain Lake, where students will get off their yellow chariot and transfer to one going to Indian Lake Central School. High schoolers have done this relay since 1949, seventh and eighth graders since 1954. Now the third, fourth and fifth graders—all three of them—will join the commuters.

Raquette Lake built a new union free school in 1973 for forty-some pupils; the most it served was about half that. Enrollment has been dropping for years, but the community has truly supported the endeavor even as the student body of fifteen in 1993 dwindled by eighty percent by 2005. The school's budget last year was $360,000.

Discussions were passionate in public meetings, the general store, the Tap Room, anywhere in the town of about 125 registered voters. To lose a school—even if it appears to be the logical economic choice—is to remove a defining portion of a place and sever a vibrant connection that binds generations; it's more than a symbolic gesture indicating there are too few young families in town. Closing a post office or shutting down a volunteer ambulance squad are other scenarios that coldly, statistically, point to demographic change. These actions could be taken as clinical observations, but they constitute a far deeper dent in the identity of a settlement.

The transition from a town that works, with residents employed in all kinds of jobs, to a town viewed as a place to play, with no lights in the windows on a dark October night, is one that's hard to resist. Like any trend, this one is driven by outside forces, not the hopes of folks who've been there all along or who have come to stay. How can a cash-strapped Adirondack town in a desirable and beautiful setting shut out real money from somewhere else? That's the irony at the heart of the situation: the tax base for the Raquette Lake school is huge because of the valuable summer homes. But rising real estate prices mean that affordable housing is somewhere else, not down the tree-shaded lane.

There will be no squeaks as shoes run across the gym floor, no slams of locker doors, no more Pledge of Allegiance this September. But the now-technically-inactive district will stay alive, with a few part-time employees; the school will maintain standards outlined by the New York State Department of Education. This move may seem like begging for life support when the patient is for all intents deceased, but it's a way to cling to the hope that someday the teachers and principal and two classrooms will find a reason to be back in session. Once a district closes, the state regards it as gone forever, and Raquette Lakers don't want someone else to make that decision. The facility will be open to the community as a place for meetings, workshops and other activities.

That Raquette Lake held on to a school this long (since the 1890s) is proof of tenacity. In the 1960s Blue Mountain Lake and its western neighbor had plenty of students in one-room schools. But Blue Mountain Lake joined Indian Lake's central school in fall 1964; when the time came to consider sending students down the road to Inlet or Old Forge, or to Long Lake, which is the political center for Raquette, residents chose instead to build a new facility with a multipurpose room, nice classrooms, offices and a large field for softball and soccer.

On June 15, Raquette Lake's Heritage Day, teacher Sue Norris was presiding over scores of visiting students from other schools, riding herd on twenty-five times more youngsters than usual. The next evening, a PowerPoint program on school history and a moving-up ceremony packed the gym, with men and women who had attended the school carrying photos of themselves in pigtails and bell bottoms or short, Peter Pan–collar blouses and dungarees. The pictures were to be scanned and saved in archives to celebrate the ordinary, a country school that taught the basics and instilled a sense of belonging, not to the larger world, but to a smaller, intensely specific place.

—SEPTEMBER/OCTOBER 2005

Totally Rad
Cast-iron arguments on the road to home heating

THE OLD HOUSE my husband and I recently bought does not appear to be haunted, but in the throes of renovating it I find myself trying to channel my dad, dead now for nine years. A mechanical engineer, he would surely have had plumbing, heating and foundation solutions in his brain, or at his fingertips in the little manuals that filled the shelves in our Wisconsin home. He could have looked at the plans, taken a slurp of bourbon and pronounced exactly how many cast-iron radiators we would need in each room, right down to the section configuration, column and fin size and length. That was the kind of problem he loved to contemplate. He also would have had a few nice heaters in the basement, just in case a person needed one.

The problem we're faced with, though, is the current local scarcity of radiators. Who knew? Sure, you can find them on eBay, but do you have any idea of what it costs to ship something as heavy as a freighter's anchor?

Our decision to go down the radiator road was triggered by a visit to a neighbor's new house, where he had stunning cherry floors milled from local logs and the most beautiful radiators painted deep, rich red. They were works of sculpture, functional art. I wanted to fill our new house with them and sit by them on cold winter nights, soaking up the steady warmth. Contrast this to the home where we currently live, where standing above a forced-hot-air duct earns a faceful of dog hair and dust, not comfort and joy.

Old cast-iron behemoths are the hot new heating trend in the North Country; every plumber I've spoken to, from Old Forge to Au Sable Forks, has assured me there's nothing better (except maybe radiant-floor heat). Once we get past the nostalgia and I ask if there are antique heaters in a warehouse someplace, I get the telephonic equivalent of head scratching. "Noo, just sold/gave/scrapped/ bartered the last ones to.... But here's his number." Or, there's a tragic tale of deliberate destruction. One local pipe pro said ruefully, "Sledgehammered a bunch two years ago. They were just too darn big to move out of the second floor." Another heating contractor commented, "It's like the poppy trade, you have to ask at the right time, you have to know somebody, you have to pass a trustworthiness test, then somebody tells you where there's a barn full of them."

So I dream of finding that dim-lit shed, packed wall to wall with glorious, intact, silent radiators, embossed with curlicues, topped with wings or shoulder blades, maybe holding a little warming oven between sections. Unpocked by rust, with nary a pinhole, they stand on peg legs ready to do an honest winter's work. There may be one that marches up a stairwell, each portion a step higher than the next, or a sweet little corner job, its delicate fins fanned like a bridge hand.

These would be in orderly lines, primed, organized in pairs and trios, with no bird droppings or mouse nests to spoil the reverie. As I said, it's a dream. We had some luck this summer in our quest. A trip to Raquette Lake scored an iron stalwart bearing a paper tag with a scribbled "Uncas" dangling from an end. Did J. P. Morgan consider this an Adirondack asset and warm his bankerly backside over it at his lakeside camp? A pair of plain janes came from the former Will Rogers Hospital, where vaudeville actors with respiratory ailments came to cure in Saranac Lake. Could these heaters have been used for a xylophone routine during a raucous night in the hospital lounge? Spritzed with seltzer by a baggy-pants clown? Or did a prolonged gurgle from the boiler launch the Niagara Falls bit, "Slowly I turn. Step by step. Inch by inch...."

In this hunt we have followed plenty of cold trails, made countless calls, driven hundreds of miles and seen many radiators. Mostly tall tubular institutional ones, the kind that evoke art class and the urge to splatter paint on the heater both to hear it hiss indignantly and to add a mark to all the previous pigment planters' wishes for aesthetic immortality. Or we find "midgets," compact and perfect for a bathroom but useless anyplace else.

Though this has turned into a peculiar hobby, we are sure that the right radiators are still out there somewhere. The frugal nature of Adirondackers means that truly useful and portable household goods stay in circulation and rarely head for landfills. This is a great practice, recycling and reusing until items just wear out. This is why we have a couple of bathroom sinks in our barn, just in case we need them in the new place. Or, they might come in handy when someone wants to trade for a good hot-water radiator. There's a particularly cute oval wall sink, with faucets and all, and it could definitely be worth one small radiator, pound for pound.

—COLLECTORS ISSUE 2006

Profit and Loss
Heritage to the highest bidder

AMONG ARCHANGELS, GABRIEL stands out, his trumpet blasting. Among Adirondack angels—and there aren't many—a certain Gabriel also stands alone. Formerly atop Crown Point's White Church, the iron giant survived eight gunshots, four different congregations, a devastating fire that destroyed the chapel and a daring burglary that plucked him from his lofty perch one dark night in 2003. The 1822 weather vane's portrait was posted on stolen-art Web sites across the world, and even Interpol was on the lookout for this treasure of Adirondack craftsmanship. The missing weather vane was so well documented, made from local ore by a local blacksmith, that its value soared.

There was a happy end to that episode: about a year after the icon disappeared it was brought to an antiques dealer in Connecticut who knew exactly where it came from; the proffered merchandise was as hot as the iron the moment it came off Henry Foster's forge. Gabriel returned home, then took up temporary residence in the Shelburne Museum, in Vermont, in 2006, where thousands of visitors admired him in the round barn, a key object in a weather vane exhibition called "Silhouettes in the Sky." Jean Burks, chief curator, sighed, "He was spectacular."

When the time came for Gabriel to cross Lake Champlain, the White Church board members knew he couldn't go back to his home in the clouds. Joan Hunsden, Crown Point historian, said, "He was too fragile." And too valuable. The committee also knew not to tempt fate again, that replacing their treasure on the roof would simply invite another disappearance.

Hunsden wondered where would be the safest place around. She is involved with the Penfield Museum, a few miles from Crown Point, but the security at that nineteenth-century Ironville homestead is decidedly not state of the art. Then it came to her—the county clink. Essex County was building a new facility in Lewis, and the defunct cells in Elizabethtown, with sturdy bars and nearby staff, had room. So this 185-year-old did time in solitary confinement. He never complained about the food or the mattress. He just endured, a six-foot-long winged specter riddled with bullet holes.

Time does not stand still, even for an angel in jail. After the first stories of Gabriel's 2003 heist were published in newspapers and ADIRONDACK LIFE, offers to buy the artifact trickled in to the White Church. Ten thousand dollars. Then more. And more. The committee had an inkling of what this folk art might bring on the open market, but when a solid six-figure bid came in, it was the proverbial offer they could not refuse.

"We thought that money could do a lot of good in a little town like Crown Point," Hunsden said. The church needs repairs, cemeteries are neglected, and cash for projects like these is scarce. A bake sale every day until Gabriel blew his horn would never equal the price a collector was willing to pay. It was a true dilemma to part with a priceless piece of the community to benefit other, smaller pieces of the community.

Now an Adirondack treasure is headed to a private home. Where is a closely kept secret, though some suspect a high-profile collector like Ralph Lauren could be the purchaser. The man who facilitated the sale is unwilling to share the information. And the price? A news item in the Plattsburgh *Press-Republican* in December put it at $750,000. Whether the committee received a king's ransom whose interest alone could support countless programs and properties is irrelevant, some historic preservationists argue. "When old buildings and landmarks vanish, our communities lose something with intrinsic value beyond the dollar," said Lake Placid resident Mark Wilcox, a passionate observer of the changing landscape. "Each time this happens we lose a little more of our sense of place, pride and self-esteem. Short-term gains are so short they are insignificant, while preserving our built environment would make long-term economic sense."

This conversation is nothing new. What is found here—ancient forests, small towns blessed more with honesty than quaintness, buildings that reflect the merging of nature with roof and walls—has tremendous value, but the resources to support these are not native. The money, in virtually all cases, comes from somewhere else. With that, a small bit of ownership is relinquished, and what a community once saw as shared property and a true expression of cultural identity goes to someone else, to hang on a wall, to alter or destroy, to salvage for another use far from its roots.

The poverty that kept simple places intact is also the heart of their undoing. Outside the Blue Line, what we have seems a bargain, whether it's an acre of undisturbed lakefront or a century-old Great Camp, an old-time pharmacy or an embellishment on a rooftop. As the story of the sale of the historic weather vane was unfolding, a grim rumor surfaced: the new owner of the Wawbeek planned to raze the centerpiece of the property, the dining building designed by architect William Coulter in 1899. This structure is a remnant of a once-celebrated Great Camp on Upper Saranac Lake, a grand complex of rustic buildings. For many years it was a popular resort but it closed in September 2007 when the land and buildings were sold to a California ad executive.

At a tag sale last fall, wall sconces and ceiling fixtures were sold, never a good sign for the future of a structure. More stories circulated, that the stones of a marvelous fireplace shaped like a tuning fork—with an intricate stairway that folded around the chimney as it led from cozy hearth to a high-ceilinged second floor with a convivial bar—were offered to a mason to rebuild someplace else. If those stones could talk what would they tell? Of engagement rings presented by the fireside, of anniversary champagne toasts. The building always belonged to the innkeepers, we all knew, but certain parts of it would always be ours.

You can't put a price on other people's memories, though those are the subtext of the countryside's biography. Certain places and things warrant respect for their part in the whole, the roles they have played, the symbols they represent. As architectural historian Mary Hotaling, of Saranac Lake, said, "It's as if another species has become extinct and the whole range of life forms is smaller, and in a way more fragile, for its lessened diversity."

Interesting, important places come crashing down, like the fabulous Dexter Lake camp, near Santa Clara, built in 1890 as a faithful copy of Albrecht Dürer's Nuremberg home, marrying Bavarian rusticity with North Country elements. Though, as Adirondack Architectural Heritage director Steven Engelhart said, "Condition is often cited as a problem when a new owner chooses to destroy an older building. But Dexter Lake was pristine." Instead of a carefully restored four-story forest mansion, demolished in 1994, there is now a huge modern house and recording studio with as much character as an office park. Ironically, when the owners, country music superstar Shania Twain and her producer husband, put the 3,000-acre estate on the market, it languished for years. Perhaps keeping the magnificent Dexter house would have garnered a quicker sale.

In Warrensburg's Pack Forest stands the Grandmother Tree, a vast white pine destined for the sawmill in 1870 to pay for some new dishes. But a greater wisdom prevailed. At her farmstead (now a demonstration forest owned by the State University of New York College of Environmental Science and Forestry) Margaret Woodward chose a living tree over a set of china, and the 300-year-old pine still shades a small clearing. Its perseverance, and the simple act of leaving it, resonates in a time when taste and fortunes dictate that anything can be bought, sold, brought down or put up.

Funny how things work here, how it's easy to save a tree, harder still to cherish an old building.

—MARCH/APRIL 2008

—SHADES OF GREEN—

Lessons From a Dead Loon
Unsportsmanlike conduct at home and at large

"I THOUGHT MAYBE you could do something about this," the conservation officer told me as he laid the dead loon on the grass. A number-four snelled hook was stuck in the bird's throat; he had drowned at the end of a fisherman's set-line off Rock Island in Blue Mountain Lake. The thirty-foot string of hooks had been left in the water at least overnight, but no lunker lake trout had taken the bait. John Ellithorpe, the officer, called the set-line "a purely illegal action," carrying a $200 fine. Killing a loon can involve state and federal penalties, but as an "animal of concern" rather than a creature on the threatened or endangered list, the feds usually take no action.

Titanium white, anthracite black—not silvery like a crow or purplish like a raven—the loon looked an elegant artist's model of a bird. His legs, set so far back, were white, with black triangles between the toes. He was heavier than a Christmas goose, and no wonder; unlike most birds, a loon's bones are solid, not hollow, so he can sink like a stone at will.

The ice had gone out a week before and our diver had just returned to his old haunts. Loons come back to the same ponds and lakes time after time, and I think this was one of a pair that made the daily circuit from Lake Durant to Blue Mountain, as predictable as church chimes. Their tremolos as they flew over the house were our Angelus, the call to begin the day.

Loons are monogamous during their lifetimes, but probably this bird had not yet begun his courtship. My neighbors had talked about seeing the loons paddling along the shore, in sheltered bays near the islands, perhaps looking for a suitable nest site. Instead of wishing for a pair of loon chicks riding on their parents' backs this summer, we can count on great strings of prolific mergansers shuttling from dock to dock.

Loon killing was a favorite pastime in the nineteenth century; the rationale was that loons ate more than their fair share of trout. Never mind that dynamite for blasting fish out of the water found its way into more than a few tackleboxes, or that sportsmen prized cigar-length trout, proudly displaying clotheslines sagging with fish.

Even William H. H. Murray wrote about the thrill of loon shooting in *Adventures in the Wilderness*. At the turn of the century along Buzzards Bay, thousands of loons were shot on their northward migration. The hunters didn't even bother to send their retrievers after the birds, leaving them to bob about in the harbor. In 1918 the Migratory Bird Treaty Act ended this slaughter. It was too late, of course, for the passenger pigeon.

Loons eat smelt, minnows, snails, crayfish, leeches, all of which may be laced with mercury, DDT, PCBs and a host of other contaminants. Remnants of DDT blocks, placed in so many streams just twenty years ago, still send their poisons into lakes. In the latest New York State Board of Health advisory, humans are warned not to eat more than one-half pound of fish caught in state waters per week. Fish from some lakes is not to be tasted, nibbled or even fed to the cat, period. What does this mean for the creatures that rely exclusively on foods from the waters?

An increasing number of Adirondack lakes support no fish, the Adirondack Lakes Survey Corporation recently proved. For five years, 1,730 water bodies were tested, and nearly a quarter of all Adirondack lakes had pH levels of five or less. That means dead. The sour sad truth is that acid rain is a problem with technological solutions in sight, but what are the incentives for another state's industries to care about a few dead lakes in a remote chunk of New York? Yes, corporations do spend money on air pollution control—about fifteen cents for every American.

The Clean Air Act was passed nearly twenty years ago, and despite increased cancer rates and significant loss of the ozone layer, we are better off than we would have been without it. President Bush's proposal for new air pollution abatement is now public. But the decision ultimately rests with Congress, which places the burden of responsibility on us. The first investment in what will be a very expensive process is just a twenty-five-cent stamp or two or three to let our senators and congressmen know that the health of the planet is worth preserving at any price.

One dead loon, a massive oil spill—it's easy to become angry when there's just one human target. We decry individual carelessness but the real problem is callousness on a national scale. What we don't care to face is that we all share the blame; we are still consumers, not yet stewards.

—JULY/AUGUST 1989

Seeing in the Dark
It's nighttime that puts heaven on Earth

CALL IT THE birth of opportunity, which is a strange thing to think while anticipating the bill for a seventy-five-mile tow and a repair tab equal to half the value of the vehicle in question. But if the fan assembly hadn't fallen off my beat-up pickup last night, I would have been fast asleep rather than audience to an hour-long celestial Cinemascope.

A pale shade over St. Huberts opposite the moonrise wasn't alpenglow. Nor was it noctilucent clouds, the night mare's tails made of meteor dust shining with reflected sunlight, but a preview to the aurora's performance. As we headed home after my ride picked me up, the night-shift animals were just coming on: russet coyote trotted east, all business in his gait, and a great horned owl went to work over the shoulder of the road, testing his tools.

Where the sky opened up west of the Boreas River, we could see streaks of lime green and wisps of pearl overhead. Usually it's radio wasteland here, but a surprising signal came in clearly — it was the calm dignity of Brahms' First Symphony, that sweeping anthem from the first movement that some call Beethoven's Tenth. Maybe the same ethers that were bringing us that spectacular display included stray wavelengths of cello,

French horn and oboe.

Hurtling down a deserted road, lights off, radio blasting, heads hanging out the window watching the sky dance is not the AAA-approved way to drive an Adirondack highway, but nothing ventured, nothing gained, right?

We stopped at the overlook by Kempshall Mountain. By now there were blue swirls at the zenith, green curtains folding and fluttering to the west, and the Big Dipper, huge, followed the contours of the hillside just skimming the horizon. Directly above Kempshall's hump, the North Star swam in a gauze of red aurora. For twenty minutes, long after the last note of the orchestra had faded, the iridescent glaze of the sky-bowl shimmered. The dogs enjoyed the night in their way, charging into the woods barking at bogey-bears and running back to us looking over their shoulders, tails wagging at their joke. Their noise brought us back to earth on the road's gravelly shoulder. By the time we pulled into our driveway, shreds of color still hung above the points of the spruce trees.

The time when we begin to pull our horizons closer, head indoors, set our sights on the mundane (storm windows and wood piles: the things that are November) is coming on fast. September's gaudy colors are well on their way to becoming next year's humus under the frozen mud, and October's tamarack gold and downy cattail beige have long washed downstream. We leave the woods to the hunters, waiting for real winter's good snow and hard ice rather than try to enjoy drizzle and wind. We balance the checkbook and put the trail maps away.

But late fall's earlier nights provide high drama without cutting into human hibernation time, and more bright stars shine now and in the winter than in other seasons. In the cold air, their light flickers so that the usually static sky scene is alive with minute motions, blinks and twinkles.

Venus, the Earth's twin in size and mass, gleams brightest of all just above the horizon as the sun sets. Jupiter can be found around midnight in the constellation Gemini (inside the hole if you think of the sky as a doughnut), and with binoculars you can see the brilliant giant's four largest moons. There's no better time to appreciate the cobbled creek of the Milky Way stretching across the sky. In November, the Andromeda Galaxy is almost directly overhead, a small eraser smudge in a vast blackboard. It is so very far away that all the energy of its hundred-billion suns is only barely visible to us. Six million acres seem puny and fragile in contrast.

Most of us can find a dozen wildflowers, identify a bird from a silhouette or tell a trout from a bass, but many of us have forgotten the names of the stars, the shapes of the constellations, the placement of the planets. We're blinded by the night, and it takes the transitory splendor of an aurora to jar us back into an appreciation of the heavens.

Around any bend of an Adirondack river may be a glimpse of terrestrial grandeur, and we may be lucky enough to have looked down on the clouds from a mountaintop, but looking up on a frosty sight is a lesson in humility. In our urgency to love a piece of land, we forget the sky from which we fell.

—NOVEMBER/DECEMBER 1989

Night School
Small fry discover the meaning of life

THE SMELT RUN when the shadbush blooms, said one old-timer. Two weeks after the ice goes out, added another. That first springtime when we lived "pret near" the lake, in a mobile home, we learned that the real sign of the annual smelt run was when cars and trucks started cruising our dead-end road well after dark.

Months had gone by without a single unfamiliar vehicle passing our house. One May night, about eleven, we heard the alien clomp of size-twelve swampers on the stoop and a knock to wake the dead. At the door I squinted in the glare of the porch bulb. "Hey," the hulking silhouette said. "Is this where the smelt run?" pointing down our bowling alley of a hallway. I muttered, "Not in here they don't," and shut the door.

The next night a carnival was going on at the end of the road. We could see the light from the Coleman lanterns that seemed to float through the woods and hear the clink of cans in the coolers as their bearers shuffled toward the shore. Since we couldn't sleep through their noise and the growling, whining and woofing of the dogs, we decided to check out the party downstream.

I'd been smelt fishing a few times before, with a long boom off a jetty in Lake Michigan. The umbrella net we used was as big as a bedspread, and when we pulled it above the waves, scores of ruler-size fish shimmied in the light of our bonfire. There was a trick to all that dropping down and hauling up: if you pulled too fast, the net would spring up as it broke the surface, and the fish would disappear back into the black water.

Here, though, was a different scene: There were no strings of bonfires on mile-long concrete piers. Smelt fishing in the Adirondacks was cozy clusters of men, mostly, huddled beside narrow brooks illuminated by flashlight and gaslight hung from the trees. Coolers were for sitting on and supplying the fuel for a long night of talking. The fishing tool of choice, a wire net, was no bigger than a collapsible salad basket.

Not that you even needed a net. The smelt filled the shallow stream, swimming dozens deep. We grabbed at them in the shallow water, pulling out fistfuls of pinky-size fish until our hands got too cold. A few yards upstream and down, other people's pails were brimming.

You did, however, need a fishing license. If you were caught without one, we were told, why, they could take away all your fishing gear, even your car! Since our only equipment was a peanut-butter bucket, we weren't overly concerned, but we did get licenses the next day.

Good thing, too. Stumbling toward the brook the next night, I bumped into an old shed. I was startled to spy a pair of eyes looking back at me from behind the antique gas pump. Slowly, an index finger moved to a pair of lips to form the universal librarian's sign. I beat feet toward the lake, wondering if cabin fever was especially virulent for people who lived in trailers.

When I got to our stretch of the stream, I said, not very loudly, "There's a guy hiding in the shed over there." A veteran smelt dipper told me, "He's the game protector. You're not poaching, are you?" With that, we drank to the mental health of men who got paid to lurk in the bushes.

After several hours of smelt snatching, we went in to clean our catch. The process is as tedious as sewing buttonholes: snip the heads, snip the tails, slit the bellies. On the newspaper lay a lost generation of would-be swimmers. The butterflied fishlet that remained was no bigger than a french fry. We stuck them in the freezer, hoping some day to accumulate enough for a meal. The next week, after a successful night, a fellow fisherman invited us to his cabin for a real Adirondack smelt fry. He mixed cornmeal, salt, pepper, eggs and beer in a bowl, dumped in anatomically whole fish and spooned them—gooey globs of them—into the bubbling lard. Peering into the pot, I could see sad little fish faces bobbing around and lost my appetite.

I still go smelt fishing these nights in early May, not for the sport, but more to witness a process that's older than dirt. What a mystery, that something as minuscule as a smelt brain responds to moonlight on the water, the push of lake and pull of stream. It's a traditional tune, and something—the tenth balsam needle to fall in the brook or the footstep of the first fawn—is the cue for the smelt.

Weeks later, when the wake robin and witchhobble have faded and blackflies are in ascendancy, the rocks are still littered with smelt corpses, too far gone and too abundant for the crows and the mink. But in pools of water, tiny smelt feed, taking notes on the stream that will call them a lifetime from now.

—MAY/JUNE 1990

Paths of the Paddlers
Exploring the Miami and Jessup Rivers

THE MAJOR HASSLE with most canoe trips has nothing to do with water. It's the car shuttle that causes the headaches: spending the energy and time to leave a vehicle where the trip will end up, and then, after a full day or more of paddling, driving back to the put-in to retrieve your other car. But using just one vehicle, leaving it at the starting point of a trip and hitchhiking back to it afterward, is a chancy proposition—you could wind up feeding generations of mosquitoes before anyone comes along.

Canoeing out and back along the same route is one solution; it might just be possible for a chain-lake trip, but it may not work at all for a river excursion. The best bet is to discover a loop or wishbone-shape trip by studying topographic maps: then one vehicle, strategically parked, solves the shuttle problem.

We didn't have a circle tour in mind, exactly, on the morning in June when we paddled the Jessup River into Indian Lake. My partner and I are mostly lake paddlers, used to the comforting sight of islands and the flat, blue horizon delineated by ridges and mountains. But this time we wanted the cool, shadowy intimacy of a small, wild river and the chance to explore a less-traveled part of a big lake.

The histories and guidebooks don't have much to say about the Jessup. The river was named for the two eighteenth-century brothers who were the real investors for Totten and Crossfield's Purchase. Verplanck Colvin listed the stream as a tributary of the Upper Hudson and estimated its length at about thirty-six miles. Alec Proskine's *Adirondack Canoe Waters, South and West Flow* mentions that the river is navigable, but on one critical map, the Jessup is mislabeled as the Indian River.

Looking at the Jessup from a topo-map perspective, the river stairsteps north and east out of a lonely quartet of ponds deep in the West Canada Lakes Wilderness Area, flowing past Perkins Clearing, joining the outlet of Whitaker Lake and emptying into the southernmost bay of Indian Lake. Scouting the river from that map, we saw that the ten- or twelve-mile trip we had planned lay in a fairly flat valley, without falls or dams to carry around and with no steep contours that would indicate rough water.

We put in at the bridge on Route 30, about six miles north of Speculator. The river there is about twenty feet wide and flows in graceful arcs between mudbanks pocked with deer tracks. There's a bit of current, enough to send leaves and sticks downstream at a brisk clip, but it doesn't sweep a boat away at a scary pace. (There are tag alders and trees along the bank, and at times, branches do fall into the river. Steer clear of these because, even in a sweet river like the Jessup, water pressure builds around these strainers, and a canoe can become trapped in a dangerous situation.)

After nearly a mile of curves and oxbows, the river widens and becomes straighter. Soon we heard the bubbling sound of shallow whitewater as the river opened up between the birches into a champagne boulevard of Class I and II whitewater. The water was low, so we stopped to scout a course, looking for the tongues (unobstructed water) between the pillows (rocks covered by smooth-flowing water) and over the ledges. Our friends, in pack canoes, slipped through like otters, but our boat, an eighteen-foot touring canoe, had just a bit too much draft. Another eight inches of water would have been ideal to float the two of us, but instead I ended up hiking through the ferns to meet up with my partner after a half mile or so.

The Jessup gradually becomes a slender five-mile-long bay of Indian Lake, with state land on both sides. Set between two ridges, and ringed by pines and spruces, it's the closest thing to a fjord you'll find in the central Adirondacks. Every mile or so along the eastern shore there are lovely little patches of sand beach, at Dug Mountain Brook, the Chocolate Bar, Woodland Brook and John Mack Landing. They're designated state campsites administered by the Indian Lake Islands Campground.

We dawdled our way up the lake, exploring Dug Mountain Falls (just a short hike off the water), poking into pocket bays, drifting from sunlight to shadow, swimming, trolling, lily-dipping. Through the entire day we saw just one other party, a couple of college kids who had come down the Jessup from Perkins Clearing, taking out sweepers and deadfalls along the way. We circled Long Island and headed southwest, past Poplar Point, to take out at Route 30, and we sent our designated walker back to the car, about four miles away.

The guidebooks don't have much to say about the Miami River, either, which drains into Lewey Lake, just across the road from our Jessup River take-out point. The Miami's source is along the Old Military Road that goes from Sled Harbor to Cedar Lakes, and it flows southeast, joining the Mason Lake outlet, then northeast into Lewey Lake. This is backcountry now, but the map of the area is peppered with names like Camp 10, Camp 19, Camp 22—all lumber outposts from the early part of the century.

We explored the Miami on a warm late-fall day. The leaves were down, baring the rolling ridges, and the rumpled contours of Snowy Mountain were graphically reflected in the still water. Lewey Lake, about a mile and a half long, is bordered on the west by massive mountains, many of them trailless: Snowy (which does have a trail) is just 101 feet short of being a High Peak, while Blue Ridge and Lewey Mountain each top thirty-eight hundred feet. There's a large state campsite on Lewey Lake but in spring and fall the lake is very quiet. On a weekday in May or October, you might even find yourself alone.

We weren't exactly alone—we spooked a great blue heron,

which flew alongside us with deliberate, pterodactyl-like wingbeats, and then a handful of black ducks, which swam away muttering. None of them, though, led us to the Miami's channel, which was obscured somewhere in the nearly seamless beaver grass on the south end of the lake. The opening is just a nondescript break in the watery meadow. If you take a topo map and compass, and set your bearings when you're parallel to the campsite beach, you'll find it quicker than we did.

The Miami is a well-tempered river in the heart of an immense wetlands, perhaps twenty-five feet wide at first, with a few oxbows guarded by muskrat huts. We were paddling upstream, with no particular goal except to go as far as we could. Finding the channel through a maze of inlets, feeder streams and sloughs proved to be a challenge, but keeping an eye on the slim weeds growing on the bottom of the six-foot-deep river kept us honest. The current bends the weeds, so if we paddled toward the waving tips of the weeds, we knew we were going upstream. If the weeds weren't bent at all, we knew we were in a dead-end backwater.

After half a mile or so, the river narrowed to the width of a canoe length. The current became correspondingly stronger, but it wasn't difficult to paddle against. The river's kinky course, though, was a lesson in pretzel-bending.

The Miami disappeared around a hummock, then doubled back 180 degrees to provide a lovely vista of Snowy Mountain, then it twisted again and again in countless curlicues. It helped to have a well-oiled repertoire of slow sweeps (an arc stroke from bow or stern on the outside of the turn), powerful draws (a flat-bladed pull straight into the side of the boat) and smooth pries (a flat-bladed push away from the side of the boat). Since we were traveling upstream, we found that a bow rudder worked well, too, the paddle steadied off the bow to pivot the canoe around a hairpin corner. We found ourselves in tight quarters at times, but we didn't leave any canoe-bow-shape dents in the mud. Bonking from bank to bank would be a distinct possibility in a less maneuverable boat.

Besides the truly myriad turns, there were no fewer than ten beaver dams in the space of a couple of miles. Rather than get out and drag the boat over, we paddled into position facing a low spot on the dam and slipped through. Reading the water flowing over the dams was tough, though, since the sunlight was glancing off the water. At one relatively straight stretch of water, all of forty feet long, we looked up to see a doe wiggling her ears at us. She had probably grown accustomed to the shouts of "Draw left! LEFT!" and our surprised silence at the sight of a curveless section of river may have spooked her.

We stopped for lunch on a high and dry spot of spruce and balsam. My partner, dressed in drab, mud-daubed clothes, was lounging in a small clearing and a pine siskin landed on his shoulder, probably mistaking him for a log. The bird beat a hasty retreat when it realized the log was eating a ham sandwich. We wondered if the critters were always this casual on the Miami. Certainly the beavers know they're in command.

We had traveled maybe two and a half miles as the sparrow flies when we came to a fork in the river. The western one was the true course, but both channels were blocked with new, high stick-and-mud dams. The sun was starting to dip low behind Cellar Mountain, so we turned around to head downstream.

To finally go with the flow was joy itself. The current, which we had convinced ourselves wasn't all that fast, gave us a three- or four-mile-an-hour push downstream, and it was stronger on the outside of each curve. Anticipating that, each twist and turn was greeted by a slow outside sweep on the bow. Soon we fell into a rhythm of sweeps, backstrokes and draws that made the Miami, beaver dams and all, a gentle slalom course. The dams were met with a few quick back paddles to position the boat, then some power to slip through the tongue. Easy! I found myself wishing for more obstacles: this was whitewater paddling without the hazard of hitting rocks. We paddled back the way we came, the length of Lewey Lake. There are a handful of camps on the eastern shore, but smoke rising from the Galushas' chimney was the only sign of civilization. The water was almost high enough to run the concrete dam that leads to Indian Lake, but we had come through the day without a scratch, so we decided not to push our luck.

Just as we were taking out by the highway, a landlocked

salmon became airborne, leaping over the dam in a flash of silver, linking the two trips, two rivers and two lakes.

—MARCH/APRIL 1991

Natural Limits
There is no risk-free wilderness

HENRY DAVID THOREAU published a modest pamphlet called *Walking*, in the 1850s. The essay, which he often delivered as a public lecture, begins with the familiar "I wish to speak a word for nature, for absolute freedom and wildness ..." More bits and pieces have been plucked from it—"in Wildness is the preservation of the world," "all good things are wild and free," and other recognizable phrases—to become the rallying cries of the environmental movement. Recently, in rereading this classic of American nature writing, I came across a passage that struck me as strangely appropriate to the mysterious death of David Boomhower late last summer, and to the news that, on February 14 this year, his sisters had filed a notice of intent to sue New York State for "enormous pecuniary damage" as a result of Boomhower's death. Thoreau wrote: "If you are ready to leave father and mother, and brother and sister, and wife and child and friends, and never see them again—if you have paid your debts, and made your will and settled all your affairs, and are a free man, then you are ready for a walk."

Thoreau was writing of a person in charge of his own life, ready to account for his own acts. He also meant a good, long walk, and maybe he would have applauded the choice of the

Northville–Lake Placid Trail, a particularly ambitious selection for such a journey. But wrapped up in Thoreau's statement are thoughts about risks, expectations and personal responsibilities. Thoreau saw angels and light in the wilderness, but he wrote of devils, too, and he called nature "this vast, savage, howling mother of ours."

Only a select few in Thoreau's day chose to enjoy the wilds; today millions of us seek the solitude, beauty and challenge that only wild country can offer. In the comfort of our homes, we flip through magazines, such as this one, that describe adventures and special out-of-the-way places. Even the advertisements entice the reader into the outdoors—with promises that a new pair of boots can make you surefooted, or that a state-of-the-art compass can turn a couch potato into an explorer. The physical act of walking hasn't changed since bipedalism evolved, yet nowadays we can overload ourselves with gear and gewgaws, and wrap our bodies in space-age fibers that wick away sweat, repel water, insulate and breathe. But not one of these things is an antidote for bad judgment, or a talisman against bad luck.

A great number of the long trails in the Adirondacks confront hikers from the git-go with warnings and advice about changeable weather, daunting distances and lack of shelter along the route. But to many of us these are merely words emanating from some nervous, desk-bound bureaucrat. We're cloaked in competence, we think, as we set out. Modern technology helps to head us into the woods with hubris rather than with humility. Besides, we've studied the guides, heard a weather report, looked at a map. Our daily, comfortable lives give us ample protection from unpredictability. Since we have mastery over a complex indoor environment, why should we be proven vulnerable in an outdoor setting that we also think we know? And so we begin our journeys without allowing for the inherent risk and irrationality of the wilds.

Most of the time things work out. If sunny skies give way to a downpour, we get wet. If we take a wrong turn, we retrace our steps. These experiences make for great stories around the kitchen table, since we make it back to tell them, but in that way we feed the myth about the "conquerability" of nature.

Things don't always work out the way we plan, though.

David Boomhower's death is tragic; it moves us to true compassion. Yet we can't help concocting "what if" scenarios that would have produced different outcomes: What if he had been hiking with a companion? What if he had made arrangements to call in at his hike's halfway point or on a certain day? What if he had taken a stove and a week's worth of freeze-dried meals?

We wonder at what point a series of small errors reached critical mass to create a desperate situation. In our minds, we replay the hearsay and the facts—and temper them with bits of our own "woodsmanship"—and still we can't come up with a good answer.

But a good answer to the possibility of the lawsuit is another matter, and that answer must be crystal clear. The underlying notion of a suit has to do with an innocent party being injured by the bad intentions, ignorance or negligence of another. Within that framework is the assumption that the injured party was not at fault for the turn of events, that something measurable or controllable was defective. In the Boomhower case, charges are being leveled that the month-long search was not conducted properly and that the trail itself was "unsafe, unreasonably dangerous and defective." Not that David himself got tired or hungry or wet or confused.

On the long wilderness walk he chose to take, David Boomhower confronted more than he bargained for, and nature does not negotiate.

—JULY/AUGUST 1991

Fish Shtick
A tale of mistaken identity

FOR A COUPLE of years I gave up on fishing. My fishing partner, an elderly neighbor, had died, and with him went all the luck I had had on the waters. After he was gone everything I tried was scorned openly by bass, walleye, even bullheads, a far cry from those mornings when we netted as much as we wanted. We'd sit in a boat tied up to the same buoy he had baited for half a century and catch the great-grandchildren of the ones that had gotten away from him during the Depression. Getting fish was peripheral, though, to the talk about fish, guides, a lifetime in the woods. I listened; occasionally a story would be punctuated by a jerk on the line, and the tale would end with a flopping fish in the boat. My friend would always take my fish off the hook, bonk it on the head with a miniature baseball bat, stuff it in a gunnysack and throw the sack under the seat, all in one fluid motion. It occurred to me much later that maybe that odd ritual had a bit to do with taking fish in all seasons in order to feed a large family.

Fishing was far from my mind on the day before Thanksgiving. That Wednesday was warm, bright, breezy, a welcome change after weeks of autumn drear. A hike was in order, up a little nubbin with a fine view of the lake. After a mile or so on the trail it was obvious that I had found the ultimate source of the Raquette River, which had chosen the footpath I was on for its route to the sea. Muddy is too tepid a word for the condition of the trail; it was a sucking quagmire. Heading down the mountain as the sun dipped westward, I was disgusted that I had wasted the season's last good day.

As I drove along, rounding the curve toward home, I glanced toward the lake. From the highway, even cruising at thirty miles an hour, I could see that the water was boiling with fish. I recalled that my friend had said that the lake trout come in late fall to spawn over gravel bars. He had never mentioned this particular location, but then no fisherman ever tells all, no matter who he's telling it to. There was only one thing to do—seize the day, at least what was left of it.

I scrounged up an old pack rod and a reel filled with questionable line, a couple of lures rescued from junk drawers. I could still see the fish in my mind, had to hit the lake before it was too late.

I parked on the side of the road, oblivious to folks heading home from work, and put my gear together. With my first cast, a newish sinking something-or-other sailed off into the sunset. Hastily I tied on a lure that was the size and color of a gherkin; it had ancient bite marks on it, a good sign, I thought.

Whammo! A fish hit immediately and headed for the next county with a mouthful of hook. I could tell this was a righteous fish, maybe the biggest one I'd ever had on a line. The rod bent double as the fish sinuously raced in, out, up, down. Zigging. Zagging. Then I noticed I didn't have a net. Hmmm.

I landed him the only way I could, by horsing him onto shore. Then I had a large, muscular, angry fish out of water. I tried to hold him down. Both hands just weren't big enough, so I had to straddle him; I could see I'd never get the hook out. I broke the line, tossed fish and lure into the back of my truck and rigged up again.

Bam! Another strike, just as powerful as the first, maybe more so. The rod curled into an upside-down J, the line's tension relaxed ever so slightly, and the rod flew apart into its four eighteen-inch-long sections, like a lively set of giant nunchakus.

It is very difficult to land a fish when the pole is in little pieces. I pulled the line in hand over hand, dragged the fish up on the beach; it wriggled back to the water. I tackled it and got my glove stuck in one of the treble hooks. Now fish, pole pieces and my gloved hand were locked in a spasmodic struggle; I got my hand out, grabbed the fish by the tail and threw the whole mess into the bed of my truck. It sounded like a troupe of bad tap dancers back there as I headed toward home.

In the clinical light of my kitchen I laid out the fishy pair—complete with glove, beach gunk and tangled line—next to a yardstick. Twenty-one inches long, maybe four pounds apiece.

My husband arrived home and inquired as to where I'd gotten the fish. I said I caught them; he didn't believe me. And when I said something about lake trout in the shallows, he laughed. I think he said something like, "Those fish are not lake trout," and he paused before he asked something like, "How many people saw you fishing?"

Well...

A careful look through a handy guide to the fishes, and a lengthy study of the New York State angling syllabus, confirmed that I had indeed pulled the wrong fish out of the wrong lake—for November, at least.

We destroyed some of the evidence for Thanksgiving dinner, and on Christmas Eve, a number of friends, including the local Forest Ranger, remarked that the poached salmon tasted wonderfully fresh. I said it was a recipe I got from an old friend.

—NOVEMBER/DECEMBER 1992

The Bird in the Hand
A hum-dinger of a true story

A WORD HERE for all the small, homely things that live in the woods, for the dust-colored female hummingbird that yo-yos up and down in the honeysuckle, for the thumbnail-size peeper that trills in the trees. The winter wren, a mousy little bird that could hide in the shadow of a puffball, gives us the loudest, sweetest song of the Adirondack spring, a brilliant cadenza of arpeggios and trills, as if all the bird's meaning were distilled in that dazzlingly clear tune.

There's mystery and vibrant force packed in the tiny things that surround us in forest and stream, those furtive scurries through the brush, silver flashes in the brook and hasty glimpses of fur, feather and fin. We tend to overlook these bits, or consider them as mere footnotes to the text, but they are as vital to the whole as any other, far grander part.

One July, for a brief period of human time, my life intersected with the life of something extremely small. (I suppose in terms of the creature's life span, the time we spent together was significantly longer.) I had just found an old scythe, in good working order, while excavating a cellar. I took a few practice swings to test its balance and sweep, then set out to mow.

On my first full arc into a ragged clump of goldenrod growing near our woodpile, the stems sliced neatly as planned, but a high, piercing *squeak!* came out of the toppled plants. Great, I thought, I nailed a nest of rabbits. But that didn't quite make sense—the time and place were all wrong. Gingerly I parted the sticks and leaves, expecting to find a furry terrestrial of some kind, a jumping mouse or a vole. Instead I found a grass-green birdlet, impossibly minute but fiercely alive: a ruby-throated hummingbird.

I don't buy lottery tickets, figuring that the odds of any isolated event are far, far greater than my winning millions of dollars, but I did think about the mathematical probability of that singular occurrence, hitting a small flying object with the blade of a farm implement. The likelihood of an osprey delivering a sky-diving trout into my canoe was probably greater. But there was a payoff for this particular random event, a chance to turn dumb luck into observation into understanding.

I picked up the hummingbird. Truly, it weighed nothing. I could feel the texture of feathers, but there was absolutely no sensation of mass, no heft to the shape. Its body parts were fine and fragile; its claws were curled into "g" shapes, smaller than the tiniest letter on this page. Its legs were thinner than thread, but far more complicated than any simple spun fiber, because within that threadlike diameter lay skin, muscle, arteries, ligaments, bones, all in exquisite order.

I cobbed a cardboard box into an ersatz shelter, with a screen on one end for light, and lined it with dry grass and some sticks for perching. The bird seemed dazed, but I couldn't find any obvious damage, and it rested quietly. I found a recipe for hummingbird nectar in a natural-history guide and poured it into a red jar lid.

A day passed. The nectar seemed untouched; the bird whistled loudly. Hungry, I figured, and I cast about for some other way to feed it. I put in some flowers. No response. The nutritional demands for something so small are proportionately huge—about like an average person shoveling in a cheeseburger every waking minute—and the possibility of starving the flightless, weightless bird I was trying to fix seemed quite real.

A friend hit on the solution: fill a small syringe with the sweet fluid and put the bird's beak into it. We were astounded. On the first try, the bird lunged voraciously, lashing a dancing, forked tongue into the tube; that strange black filament seemed longer than its entire body. We fed the bird nearly nonstop for several days as it gained strength. One morning the bird greeted me with a miniature elevator routine, buzzing up and down in the box, and we thought the time had come for it to go back into the world.

In the meantime, my curiosity had grown. I couldn't believe that this was an adult hummingbird, although its coloration could have been that of an adult female. It was too darn small. Its behavior was just too infantile. The usual field guides weren't particularly helpful. Most described an adult hummingbird as about three or four inches long, but in hummingbird scale an inch either way is a vast difference. "Pugnacious," summarized one reference in describing ruby-throat behavior. That much I knew already; this was one fierce fledgling.

As luck would have it, a friend happened to have a male ruby-throated hummingbird in the freezer. This specimen looked like a real stud, the amazing hulk, compared to the midget bird in my laundry room.

I learned more. I had wondered why I couldn't feel a heartbeat when I had held the bird, and discovered that since a hummingbird's heart thrums at the rate of about twenty-one times a second, my crude hands probably just couldn't sense something that quick. As the bird grew stronger, I read about the epic journey he or she would make from these mossy damp woods to the sunlit jungles of Central America, some 3,000 miles, with a 500-mile nonstop crossing of the Gulf of Mexico. That a creature so tiny should determinedly travel such a great distance was proof of immeasurable strength. Knowing how, where and when to go seemed beyond the greatest technological triumph: this bird's brain was programmed with far more complicated information than any microchip I had ever met.

Then I released it. The bird helicoptered up, then turned tail, and I swear it flew upside down before peeling off into the distance. As I watched the tiny ruby-throat disappear, I wondered why it is that we always seek out the big stuff, the "-est" things—

highest, longest, largest. There's an unseemly measure of competitiveness in our observations and opinions of the wild world; witness the overwhelming popularity of the tallest of the High Peaks, when other, lesser climbs have equally excellent views. Old growth is hot now, with folks irresistibly drawn to stately white pines, forgetting that there are equally ancient—but knee-high, twisted—spruce on the mountainsides. A dreadful Newspeak phrase summarizes our inherent attraction to moose, wolves, mountain lions and such—"charismatic megafauna."

Instead, I say here's to the awesome power of three grams of hummingbird muscle and the sustained song of an invisible wren.

—JULY/AUGUST 1993

A Season Apart
The lingering spell of summer

ROUND ABOUT NOON on Labor Day the best part of the year begins. Some local folks have a tradition of commemorating the day by waving farewell to southbound motorists, gathering in a rowdy clump at a parking pull-out by the Hudson River on Route 28. Countless school systems try to prove the calendar wrong by stealing away the last weeks of summer. With the first diesel roar of the bright-yellow buses they dictate that fall has begun. Anyone who's lived more than a year in the Adirondacks is outwardly willing to acknowledge that lie, but deep down this is the season we've been waiting for all along.

For nine months we've been penitent and patient, enduring cold, snow, ice, mud, heat, bugs, crowds, bugs, heat, crowds and more bugs. Winter gets tiresome when it enters its seventh month; spring wavers between a cruel hoax and a fleeting tryst; vacation season—bracketed by the Fourth of July and the first of September—is so maniacally packed with things to do, places to go, people to see, that by August summer starts to look and feel like the worst kind of frat-party weekend, with blackened bones of chicken barbecues appearing, wraithlike, from the dim recesses of the refrigerator, grim reminders of all chores left undone. Then, it's all over—the hubbub, I mean—but blessedly, a precious sliver of decent weather remains as a reward.

Suddenly quiet reigns, and along with it come dry, sunny, warmish days and starry, mosquito-less nights. The water is still fine swimming, and there's no need to feel self-conscious about sporting that definitive North Country tan: arms brown up to the elbow, left one darker than the right. Finally tomatoes are ripe; the grass has stopped growing. The woodpile has turned a splintery bleached gray, but what it signifies seems remote indeed.

Up high on the mountain I expect I'll find a certain patch of blackberries that will have escaped the ravages of she-bears and cubs. The thick canes are brutally spiked, all the better to guard enormous, winey fruit. I'll take along my elderly, white-whiskered dog; she enjoys berries even more than I do, gently slipping ripest ones from the branches she can reach. Like a small furry tank, she will plow determinedly into the worst brambles, only emerge with twigs plastered to her ears and a lolling telltale deep-purple tongue. These are the days for recapturing the summer's all-too-popular spots, now deserted. On the pond behind the mountain, I plan to be the first paddler of that secret season, the only paddler, caught on water so still that sky, cliff, tree and bank all meld seamlessly in endless repetition. Last fall I headed out on a smooth, bottomless stream that comes from a pond the next ridge over. When I stopped to drift, the river's perfect picture had lost all its margins and references, and I could not truly tell sky from water. In my leaf-color, leaf-shape boat I wove between the spectral hemlock branches, mesmerized.

There's a steady reassurance to the weather, the fitful winds and tumultuous storms left behind. I can watch Blue Mountain collect a lens-shape cloud cap on its lee side, which benignly scuds away without a drop. The peaceful late-summer dusk has a cool, soft feel, so distinctive it ought to have its own terminology.

The black-faced doe is bolder now, having spent two months in swamp seclusion. She leads a couple of bumbling round-headed yearlings—daughter and niece, probably—and this year's fawn, spots now blended and nearly as tall as the doe, out into the field at twilight. Each night another deer or two joins the troupe, with a buck emerging last of all from the edge of the woods. Even without antlers (his thick velvet-covered nubs usually don't appear until mid-September), he looks different, much deeper through the chest and stockier in the neck, than the does. He acts differently too—imperious, nervous, self-important—stamping and blowing as his casual harem meanders through fetlock-high thyme.

These are the very same deer, mind you, that I curse roundly throughout June, July and August for their guerrilla-style garden attacks; by now, all is forgiven. Summer's slow fade is marked not only by the changing leaves, but by the deer's color shift from coppery buff to steel gray. I know the season's over when they've all grown thick blankets against the coming cold, and the buck's antlers cast shadows echoing bare branches yet to come.

—SEPTEMBER/OCTOBER 1993

Turning Turtle
An ancient, muddy migration marches on

OF ALL THE spring migrations—the high, honking strands of geese in April, the bright-colored burst of warblers in May—the oldest trek of all is the least celebrated, hardly even noticed, in fact. Out of the mud they trudge, the sturdy, determined turtles of lake and forest, heading toward the warmth, for love. There's a road I travel with clockwork regularity, so I tend to notice minutiae as a way to escape the routine. One damp but fine morning I spied an oval brown lump planted precisely atop the highway's yellow line; this rock had no business being there, I thought, as I slowed down to investigate. Sure enough, a head poked out, then four square, stumpy legs, as the turtle prepared to cross the pavement. It moved briskly, its shell clunking down noisily at every step.

This, I later learned, was a wood turtle, a solitary reptile of the Adirondack woods. Tortoise-shape walker rather than streamlined swimmer, she was about the size of a dessert dish, with shocking flame-orange skin and a high, arched shell of crenulated concentric plates that flared out into a skirt. The animal was headed for a sandy bank that also happened to be the village softball field. I drove off; I didn't want to witness her laying eggs at home plate.

A few miles farther on I stopped for another wood turtle. This one was smaller, almost bird-like in demeanor, with round, intelligent-looking eyes and a gently rounded beak. She seemed harmless, friendly even, so I carried her across the road and left her in some damp leaves. After a night of steady rain, the day's steamy sunlight appeared to be triggering a mass migration, propelling females to find just the right combination of pliant ground, shelter and whatever else it is that accumulated turtle knowledge tells them is a good spot to start the next generation.

Closer to home, the snappers were moving landward after thrashing lustily about in the shallows, appropriating sandy canoe carries and old roadbeds for nurseries. I saw them crossing busy highways and marching down hiking trails. One Saturday my dog took off into our woods and began barking hysterically. From the concentrated racket I could tell that she wasn't moving, and with an expectation of the worst—a cornered porcupine or skunk—I went to the rescue.

All the commotion was about a most peculiar sight: a big snapping turtle resolutely stuck in a brittle, rusted-out iron kettle barely bigger than its mossy shell. This was an odd place for a nest, a dank, shady hillside littered with the remains of an old dump—broken bottles, fossilized shoes and crumpled cans poking up through the duff. Perhaps a smart place to leave youngsters, though, since it was close to a house with two large dogs, which might discourage would-be predators, and near a small stream that little turtles would find just the right size. The muddy trickle was full of tadpoles, slugs and rotting plants, which would provide a slimy smorgasbord.

Old turtle hissed, extending her neck an awesome, threatening distance, so we left her alone. I returned to the spot some months later, hoping to find some hatchlings, but I was either too early—they hadn't broken out of their leathery ping-pong balls yet—or too late—a fox or coon had eaten the clutch—or I was in the wrong place. Many turtles dig false nests, perhaps to lure hunters away from the real site.

On another May day, while I was exploring a nearby pond, I

found a painted turtle firmly installed in the center of an old logging road. She had an air of concentration, her backside submerged in the warm sand, so I could look closely at the delicate dashes of red and yellow on her shell and streaks of bright color on her neck. These are the turtles that stack up on logs and rocks, basking in the sun; maybe this one was laying the groundwork for her own future high-rise.

For the last two hundred million years or so, turtles have been making their way across the land every spring, striding through the shade of giant fern trees and climbing in and out of dinosaur footprints, sharing their riverbanks with great woolly mammoths and tiny horses. The Adirondacks have risen, fallen, been ground down by ice sheets and are slowly rising again; inland seas have come and gone, then filled the valleys, while rivers have drained north, then south, and carved oxbows and chasms through the bedrock. The glaciers left behind sand and gravel for perfect turtle havens, but still they keep moving when the sun unlocks their souls, their timeless boundaries shaped only by need.

—MAY/JUNE 1994

Trouble Bruin?
Learning to live with bears

THE INSOLENT YOUNGSTER first appeared in our lives at dessert time on the Fourth of July, slouching through the yard with a swivel-hipped, self-assured gait. His lank black hair glistened with grease; his deep-set brown eyes glowered an insouciant challenge. I swear that when I shouted in his direction he curled his upper lip in a sneer. From that moment, we called him Elvis.

To be sure, bears have come and bears have gone in Blue Mountain Lake. One of our pivotal north-woods experiences happened nearly two decades ago at a diner, while we watched a bear enthusiastically root through refuse piled in the back of a pickup truck. The creature's head was approximately the diameter of a thirty-gallon garbage can, and when he stood on his hind legs he towered over the cab. Gentle Ben, my foot. This was the Terminator.

Perhaps his descendants were with us in 1995. Elvis and an army of impersonators turned up everywhere, in the sand pits at twilight, on the public beach at dawn, testing their strength and cunning against every garbage shed, dumpster and allegedly animal-proof receptacle for miles around and leaving behind impressive proof of capacious digestive tracts. At the post office (especially on days when phalanxes of visitors were crowding the counter), some of us would take perverse delight in asking neighbors, "Have you seen Elvis?" The reply—something along the lines of "Yeah, I caught him last night trying to chew through my garage door"—was sure to clear the room.

The entire Adirondacks was rife with young ursines with attitude throughout the summer and fall, partly because dry conditions had produced poor bug and berry crops and because landfills—which had provided easy and ample chow for generations of freeloaders—are closed. As a result, these nomads have learned rather well to associate homes with meals. A bear apparently was responsible for the destruction of an island camp in Long Lake; while breaking into the place it knocked over the gas refrigerator, which ruptured the gas line, which was ignited by the pilot light of the stove, which set the cabin off like a Roman candle. The perpetrator seems to have escaped unscathed.

Terry Fish's family, in Indian Lake, was awakened one soft August night by a ruckus in the kitchen: A full-grown bear had come through the screen of a sliding door and slam-bammed into the house. It smashed a cake container to devour the chocolate layers inside, bumped on the overhead light with a stray paw or its nose, roughly yanked the silverware drawer apart and sent utensils clattering to the floor. At that point the beast skedaddled out its ad-hoc entrance, but not before leaving a lake-size puddle on the floor.

Bears went after barbecue grills, bird feeders packed with sunflower seeds, dishes of pet food left near doghouses, compost piles filled with rotten fruit, horse chow spilled near barns. That omnivores with a good sense of smell would be attracted to such smorgasbords shouldn't be a surprise.

In Saranac Lake a bear played "go in and out the window" at a local restaurant early one morning, but it caused only minor damage since the food was securely put away. There was a polite encounter in Long Lake when a bear bumbling on a porch swiped the doorbell and set it off. Luckily the folks peeked through the window before they answered. Trick or treat, indeed.

For every bear story there's somebody's notion about how to confront the problem. Ideas floated this summer including installing feeding troughs in accessible locations so that tourists could get the thrill of seeing bears without going to a smelly old dump; offering generous bounties to hunters; and launching jumbo versions of catch-and-release, in which numerous problem bears would be trapped and carted far away. The first would only educate creatures to become more dependent, the second is illegal and the third can't be counted on for more than a few situations: a bear from Inlet, for instance, was taken seventy miles from home and made it back in two weks.

This fall the bears are returning to deep woods to gorge on natural foods and put on thick layers of fat for the winter. Around mid-November they'll head off to their dens. While they're hibernating, we'll have time to reflect on what it means to live in bear country. There's no quick fix coming, no panacea, just small ways of altering our housekeeping. The best bet with bears is to lead them not into temptation.

—NOVEMBER/DECEMBER 1995

Bob Tale
Slithering down a slender slope

LAST JANUARY—on a day that felt like it belonged to a real Adirondack winter, not one that was borrowed from the Carolinas—I tried bobsledding. I can't say that it was something I've always dreamed of doing, that I've entertained vivid fantasies of hurtling down a concrete chute in a heavy metal device equipped with only the most primitive rudiments of speed and directional control. Nope. It was an impulse. We piled on the polypro, wool and goose down and headed off toward Lake Placid, to Mount Van Hoevenberg ...

   To stand in line at the ticket booth, scrawl our names on a couple pages of waivers, wait by the bathrooms and stand in line some more with scores of other people. The queue didn't move much; we had ample opportunity to scrutinize our fellow slider wannabes. They were clad in denim, dressy leather booties, stylish nip-waisted jackets, gloves. They had great hair, manicures, makeup, like they were going to a party. We had on insulated pacs, surplus pants from some army that actually fought cold wars, vests, jackets, mittens, hats and hoods, as if we were joining the Tenth Mountain Division for maneuvers. They talked fast out of jittery anticipation, or in order to create heat from the friction of moving parts. We took it all in.

One scantily attired fellow—wearing, I kid you not, tasseled loafers—prattled on about how bobsledding was way better than Fear Mountain or some other high-tech wonder at a sun-splashed theme park. As his jaw flapped, a sled shot by and the thin wail of a lady's voice feathered through the frigid air, "Oohhhhh noooooooo," and Dopplered off into the trees.

We shuffled our feet, thumped our hands together and hunkered down into our clothes, relieved we had the foresight to make a pit stop before we joined the line. We climbed a step or two, inching ever closer to the bob-run's halfway point, where the sleds for paying customers start. From a loudspeaker a voice droned on, calling the curves as if each sled were contending for a medal. Finally we were within a couple of slots of getting into position. We watched intently for the instructions from the driver and brakeman, hoping to get some valuable insight into what we were supposed to do when it was our turn. They mumbled, fumbled, handed out helmets. Everyone plopped down on the sled toboggan-style and they rumbled down the track.

Our turn. I checked out the duct tape on the cushion of the sled—a funky-looking number not at all like the aerodynamic fiberglass machines they show on TV—that apparently dated back before Rockefeller's days as governor of New York. I peered in the wooden box containing the helmets, which were scuffed and chipped. I tried not to imagine how they got that way. The pilot—a strong young guy who had just finished a perfect run, hauled the couple-hundred-pound sled out of the track and onto a truck, motored up the access road and unloaded the sled at the start—told us sternly to keep our hands and feet inside the sled. That's it. He sat down, we sat down, the brakeman sat down ...

Suddenly we're racing down the sluiceway just a heartbeat above the ice. The runners skitter. The sled chugs like a locomotive, then shoots like a rocket. *Wham*! A curve to the left. *Wham*! A crook to the right. The sled takes the turns like giant twitches. *Bonk*! My helmet slips over my eyes. I can't let go of my vise grip around the person in front of me, who thankfully happens to be the guy to whom I am married. I consider raising a hand to adjust my headgear but my arm seems to be frozen in place, and I decide after a split second that not being able to see is probably a good thing. The ride is all thundering noise and g-forces.

Then in a flash we're shooting up, up the wall on Shady Corner, runners and bodies perpendicular to the ground (What ground? Aren't we flying?), then down, fast, faster, the runners *clackety-clacking* and roaring all around. We zig. We zag. There's no nuance, no subtlety, just slamming brute force and white speed. Curves this way, that way. Drops. We must be going sixty, seventy. With one eye I catch the high wall of the finish curve, looks like a big sweep, but it's nothing like that, it's a long hard charge ...

Up to the ramp at the end where we lose speed, come to a stop and breathe. The crowd should be cheering, but no, sorry, it's just us, ordinary tourist types, back to reality. We're laughing, truly thrilled, joking. It's all too fast to be really scary and we're ready, each of us, right then and there, to do it again. My husband checks his watch. Elapsed time: forty-eight seconds. An eye blink. A lifetime.

—JANUARY/FEBRUARY 1996

Mood Indigo
Marking the end of the bunting season

JUST A CHANCE glance out an upstairs window and there it was, clinging to a chokecherry twig—a male bluebird, the last creature I expected to see through the driving sleet of a November gale. He picked at the shriveled fruit as the branch flailed in the wind, then, as suddenly as he appeared, veered away in a gust. I never expected to see a bluebird again; our house is ringed by scratchy thickets and dense, wet woods, not the wide-open pastures that they prefer.

But that sweet blue against dull skies stuck in my memory, and I was well pleased last spring when all the birds of color returned (some, like the goldfinches, had in truth been with us all winter; as the sun strengthened so did their glowing yellow plumage). Darting, streaky warblers in black, white, orange and chestnut were among the first migrants to arrive. This spot is theirs too; they are no less proprietary of our gone-to-brambles patches of cue-stick-diameter soft maple, whiplike blackberry canes and choking bindweed. They nest in our balsams and spruces and eat in our lilacs and honeysuckle, painstakingly harvesting minuscule insects from leaves and bark.

This spring we were startled by a newcomer, decked out in a vivid flash the shade of poppies in Kashmir or a bottomless lagoon in Jamaica, dazzling deep, tropical turquoise as bright as the starless sky before sunrise. There—right in the middle of a tall, late-to-leaf hydrangea—was an indigo bunting. Against dull sticks he glowed like neon.

For the next few weeks, always at dinnertime, he was perched there. It was impossible not to look at him, but he wasn't there as an exhibitionist, posing like a peacock. He was simply hanging out, neither feeding nor flitting, just sitting passively in a most unbirdish way. He seemed preoccupied, his thoughts miles away. We figured him to be an expectant father and imagined that tree to be his waiting room, where he flipped through outdated magazines, wrote lists he'd later lose in his pockets, stared at the clock and wished for something to happen.

That something was a small family, growing somewhere in the brush not far from the house. We never—knowingly, anyway—caught a glimpse of his lady bunting, with plumage "extremely plain brown" according to a field guide. We never spotted the pair of them hunting for beetles to take back to their brood. Though we looked from time to time, we didn't see baby buntings, either, which go from eggs to flying juveniles in just a little less than four weeks. But we know they were there.

As spring proceeded, it wasn't so much seeing a strike of blue that proved their existence; what caught our attention was the male bunting's persistent song. From a gnarled, storm-struck apple tree to the west, he declared his border; from a white birch to the north he noted a corner with intricate trills. With the precise definition of a surveyor shooting a line he sang our yard to be his home.

One August day I followed his whistle to a small drab canary crouched in the shade, and then he took off into the sun, becoming blue as heaven. It turns out, I learned, that fabulous indigo is a trick of light hitting iridescent—yet absolutely black, according to some law of physics—feathers.

Summer passed, and the bunting's song faded to a random few chirps. His ultramarine outfit changed as well, to mottled gray-brown-black-blue, the new, utilitarian coat that would carry him south. Then he was gone.

November is the season that teeters on the brink of despair, with too-short days, grim weather and winter's inevitable locking up ahead. But in all the bare branches etched in slaty skies, bird nests are visible, plentiful even, proof that they've been sharing our territory all along. Unlike the indigo bunting, they've been quiet and camouflaged, oblivious to our self-absorbed, bumptious lives.

In a maple branch overhanging the driveway, there's a mossy tangle assembled by cedar waxwings that would make Martha Stewart envious; in a head-high sapling is an exquisite beak-built basket of milkweed shreds and spider silk from a yellow warbler. A robin's muddy bowl is just a stone's throw from the front porch. Somewhere out on the edge of our woods is a neat assemblage of goldenrod stems and grass, lined perhaps with a little golden-retriever fur, nursery of the indigo buntings. In all these naked nests is hope for the next season, and the next, bringing us back to days of clear color and bright song.

—NOVEMBER/DECEMBER 1996

Woods Bound
A backyard walkabout into winter

AS THE LAST tamarack needles shimmy to the ground and the final straggling band of geese disappears beyond the hills that edge the southern horizon, I head for our woods. I've been waiting for the weather that most people dread, the hardening up, the starkness. At last I can travel freely through the trees behind our house.

All summer long, thanks to blood-sucking bugs and boot-sucking mud, the far reaches of our seven-plus acres have been off limits. This is fine for the real owners of the place: deer, raccoons, gray fox, ermine, snowshoe hare, ruffed grouse, pileated woodpeckers and chickadees, and they're no doubt thankful for the seasons of uninterrupted peace. Even in high autumn, some reaches of the land are still too soggy for humans to pass pleasantly through, and the brush remains rankly pernicious, snagging everything that goes by. When the ground freezes solid and the leaves fall, our woods puts out a tacit welcome.

To be sure, this bit of land is unremarkable. There's no sweeping vista, no pristine pond, no crystalline cliff, no brook teeming with heirloom Folwell-strain trout, no 200-foot-tall white pine slashed with the king's broad arrow, a relic from the days when New York was just another struggling colony. There's nothing much to attract the curious or invite explorers.

Like many plots in our neighborhood, this was once a farm of sorts, not with fields and silos, but a barn, a couple sheds and some livestock: a milk cow, a team, pigs, a flock of chickens. The parcel is threaded with derelict wire fencing, now puckering the bark of ten-inch soft maples that in the early years of this century were perfect posts, as tall as my head and as big around as my wrist. Past residents left numerous dumplets a respectable distance from the house, where old leather shoes, shards of crockery and jars of every shape and size poke up through the dirt. Every hard freeze seems to bring a new crop of artifacts to light. In spots—probably corners of long-gone pasture where cows and horses liked to stand—the soil's as dark and rich as chocolate cake. In other places it's treacherous ledge that roots can barely grasp.

On a north-facing hillside there's a pocket of big hemlocks that escaped the tanbarkers—too far and too few to be of any use. From that slope you could once see all the way to the lake, unimaginable now that it's thick with yellow birch, cherry, beech and witch hobble. Where the ground flattens the forest floor is lively, even after long cold nights, with bright evergreen ferns, long runners of ground pine and ground cedar and strange golden mushrooms. On a dank, gloomy day, textures (scaly pine bark, yarnlike moss) and smells (sour, sharp popple; wintergreen whiffs of yellow birch) draw me in deep.

A few Novembers ago I spent hours and days making a trail through this little plot; the result was to be a Christmas surprise for my husband—something that wouldn't wear out, get used up or look silly years from now. I took loppers, pruning shears and a lethal brush ax in hand, but my project had been helped along by a venerable path. It started out bracketed by two hemlock trunks and traversed the slope to the power line, and I think it used to be the way that long-grown children walked into town. But I didn't want to go there; I wanted to set a route for a winter's twilight walk, through our own woods and nowhere else. A place to ski, snowshoe and wander with dogs a comfortable distance away from the woodstove's warmth would suit my purposes just fine.

I took a cue from the deer, who followed the contours and packed a well-defined route into a sheltered area of balsam and tamarack. A friend dubbed this "Little Canada" because it reminded him of the treescape of northern Quebec; the trunks are spindly, nearly limbless, straight as frozen clothesline, and mesmerizing after a storm, when the snow sticks to the windward side of the trunks and the brown-and-white-striped pattern repeats endlessly so it's easy to get turned around. From that stand, a narrow old roadway meandered eastward, and it was easy to cut a connector back up the hill. Part of the trail traced the property line and cut through a picket-size clearing that sketched out a story and swallowed up the rest: a stack of decaying stumps, the rim of an old wagon wheel, a bottomless galvanized bucket.

An unexceptional place, our woods is a work in progress, subject to blowdown and new growth, driving rain and filtered sunlight. It metes the seasons succinctly, weighing time in fallen leaves and a blanket of snow.

—NOVEMBER/DECEMBER 1997

If Wishes Were Fishes
The lure of legendary Lost Pond

THAT TROUT SEASON opens on April 1 is an exquisite irony; that an angler would be foolish enough to even try for a trout then is laughable. For me, the season opening isn't a time for action, it's a time for reflection, about fishing that was, and the fishing that will be.

What most anglers look for, I submit, isn't fish—it's Brigadoon. We're looking for the perfect, memorable session in the outdoors that can never be reproduced no matter how hard we try—the moment of absolute, crystalline focus, the sense of complete involvement in our surroundings and ephemeral understanding.

Throughout Adirondack literature, the notion of the angling epiphany carries through. Reverend Joel Tyler Headley, best known for his writing about the tiny, hardscrabble community of Long Lake in the 1840s, shared his vision of the perfect fishing day: "When the sun at length totally disappeared behind the mountains and the surface of Cold River, overshadowed by an impenetrable forest, became black as ink, the trout left their retreats; in a short time the water was in a foam with their constant leaping. Where but a short time before we had passed, looking down through the clear depths without seeing a single finny rover, now there seemed to be an innumerable multitude ... I never saw anything like it in my life—it was a constant leap, roll and plunge there around our lines."

William H. H. Murray, another pen-wielding preacher, perpetuated that abiding myth of local fishing lore, the Lost Pond. In *Adventures in the Wilderness* he wrote, "We stepped into our boat and glided out toward the centre of the pool. Not a motion in the air; not a ripple in the water. At last the beeches along the western slope began to rustle.... The zephyr at length reached the lake, and the cool water thrilled into ripples at its touch; while the pool, which an instant before shone under the sun like seamless glass, shook with a thousand tiny undulations.... Now," Murray's guide said, "if the fish haven't all drowned since I was here, you'll see 'em soon."

They cast for hours, catching trout after trout weighing two pounds or more, specimens that guide John Plumley called "regular sharks," because the flies came out of their mouths bare to the shank. In Murray's words now: "Did you ever sit in a boat, with nine ounces of lance wood for a rod, and two hundred feet of braided silk in your double-acting reel, and hook a trout whose strain brought tip and butt together as you checked him in some wild flight and tested your quivering line from gut to reel-knot? No one knows what game there is in a trout unless he has fought it out.... If one should ask me what is my conception of pure physical happiness, I should assure him that the highest bodily beatitude I ever expect to reach is to sit in a boat once more upon that little lake, with John at the paddle, and match again a Conroy rod against a three-pound trout. That's what I call happiness."

Some forty-six years later, Henry Abbott brought up the legend of the Lost Pond in one of his charming Birch Bark Books. Abbott was an inventor who made a considerable fortune designing watch-winding mechanisms, and each Christmas he published a new little book about an Adirondack adventure. His 1915 gift was *Lost Pond*.

Abbott and his faithful guide Bige decided to find Lost Pond, which they were sure was somewhere up Long Lake and on the slopes of Mount Seward, and he wrote, "Giving proper consideration to the facts and knowing the Long Lake guides as well as I did, I could readily understand that it might be less strenuous to tell the marvelous stories about Lost Pond than it would be to go up in the Seward country and search out the pond. There's always the possibility that too much investigation might spoil a good story."

They paddled, hiked, hunted and searched, and found a lovely little flow that they christened Roaring Brook. Eventually they got to the source of the stream. "It was a beautiful sheet of glassy water, with the bowl tilted on one side until the water spilled over its lower edge into the brook. The pond was about two hundred yards in diameter. The water was clear and cold as ice."

They cobbled together a raft from some logs and a bit of rope and poled their boat out into the pond. Abbott wrote, "Then followed twenty minutes of the swiftest and most exciting trout fishing I have ever experienced, I could have hooked three or four at a time if I had put on that many flies, but one kept me busy. With every cast, two or three trout would make a rush for the fly, and they would fight one another for the possession of it. Even after one fish was securely hooked and was struggling for his freedom, the others would appear and try to take the fly away from him. Bige said, 'The trout climbed out, stood on their tails, and reached for the fly before it hit the water.' The fish were beautiful, muscular, colorful, like 'chain lightning.'"

Of course, the next morning the trout had vanished. Abbott and Bige fished for hours, never saw a one. Furthermore, they discovered the pond was only about three feet deep: "The shoals of trout we had seen and heard—some of which we had eaten—had disappeared utterly and completely. Bige said, 'They've gone back to the ice chest.'"

So where is my lost pond? I can't say, but I have all of March and April, our imaginary Adirondack springtime, to contemplate Brigadoon.

—MARCH/APRIL 1999

Red Wolf or Red Herring?
A closer look at the Adirondack Park's top dog

A COUPLE OF years ago—about the time that the notion of bringing wolves back into the Adirondacks was introduced, and continuing through the hours and days that wolf lovers argued passionately for them and county legislators ruled just as passionately against them—scientists in Canada began what amounts to a massive paternity suit. In the wildlife forensic laboratory at Trent University, in Peterborough, Ontario, Paul Wilson has been determining the DNA composition of some 1,500 wild canids. Among the specimens are seventy or so skulls and tissue samples collected from North Country hunters, trappers and researchers by Bob Chambers of the State University of New York College of Environmental Science and Forestry.

Chambers has been studying New York coyotes (*Canis latrans*) since 1969, primarily around Long Lake and Newcomb, where SUNY–ESF's Adirondack Ecological Center is based. In 1997 he connected with biologists working in Canada's Algonquin Park, who were taking a closer look at that preserve's top predator, the wolf.

Algonquin Park, a two-million-acre enclave of wild lakes and big forests, is north of Toronto and west of Ottawa. Its wolves are compact: males typically weigh less than sixty-five pounds (bigger beavers have been found in Ontario ponds). Both sexes are often rust-colored or brownish rather than the classic charcoal of timber wolves. For many years observers believed that the creatures were a small race of gray wolf (*Canis lupus*), which had evolved to a particular size and hue because of geographic isolation. But recent tests suggest that Algonquin wolves are reddish because they are, in fact, red wolves (*Canis rufus*—although *Canis lycaon* has been offered as the scientific name for this eastern wolf).

To further complicate matters, some U.S. scientists believe that red wolves represent a cross between coyotes and gray wolves. Based on their genetic evidence, Wilson and Brad White, at McMaster University, in Hamilton, Ontario, propose that red wolves are indeed a valid species.

Algonquin Park and the Adirondack Park have distinct parallels: both were founded in the 1890s to protect watersheds and the remaining timber; both attract millions of canoeists, campers, hikers, anglers and winter recreationists; both have a good complement of boreal flora and fauna, from loons and eagles to moose and whitetails. Add to the similarities each park's respective wild canids. What we've been calling coyotes here—maybe the old-timers were right when they referred to them as brush wolves—look an awful lot like the red wolves of Algonquin Park. According to White, the Adirondack specimens examined in the last two years "represent a range of hybrids from primarily coyote to primarily red wolf. Our belief is that they originated from red wolves and hybridized with coyotes as that species swept north over the last seventy years."

Only since 1997 has the thinking on ancestral wolf territory begun to change. The old picture had a small race of gray wolves present throughout the Northeast, ranging as far south as Delaware, when European settlement began. The Ontario team's new view points to gray wolves occupying Canada and the mountain West, and red wolves extending from the Rio Grande to the St. Lawrence River well into the 1800s. And some of those may have stayed behind.

    The Adirondack historical record is fuzzy at best. If the beast howled like a wolf and hunted livestock like a wolf, it was a wolf; taxonomy didn't much matter when the time came to pay a bounty. The earliest publication cataloging Adirondack fauna, written in the 1840s by James E. DeKay, lists a wild canine twenty-six inches at the shoulder and forty-eight inches nose to tail, which could easily describe today's Algonquin wolf. Clinton Hart Merriam, who compiled *Mammals of the Adirondack Region* in the 1880s, fails to mention any vital statistics for *Canis lupis*—except to cite the amount counties shelled out to encourage killing them.

    Is it possible that the big bad wolf (*Canis lupus*) was never really present—except for an occasional stray—in the Adirondack Park? We may be one step closer to an answer when a sample of hide and fur from the Adirondack Museum's stuffed wolf is analyzed. The animal has as well-documented a history as a detective could hope for: he was found caught in a trap on November 10, 1893, by guide Reuben Cary at Brandreth Lake. This slim, long-legged fellow was exhibited at the St. Louis World's Fair in 1903 as "the last wolf killed in the Adirondacks."

    On June 29, Ray Masters, from the Adirondack Ecological Center, removed a minute patch from the mount's left shoulder, which was sent to the Trent University wildlife forensic lab. The story's not over for Reuben Cary's wolf, and the search continues for other century-old specimens with proven Adirondack roots. Got an ancient Blue Line wolf in your house? Give us a call.

—SEPTEMBER/OCTOBER 1999

Dog Daze
Will the real Adirondack wolf please stand up?

EARLY JANUARY. YIPS, warbles and trills bounce off the hillside of this natural amphitheater. The coyotes are in grand voice tonight, cacophonous as cathedral bells. Perhaps they're celebrating, and with good reason: It looks like they're the top dogs in the Adirondacks after all.

After two-plus years of deliberation, an Adirondack citizens' advisory committee appears to have put the issue of gray-wolf restoration to rest. On December 21, 1999, their long-awaited feasibility study was released. One finding—that we already have a creature that occupies "the functional niche of a summit predator"—comes as no surprise. The study also states quite clearly that "ecological conditions in the Adirondack Park dictate against a successful reintroduction of gray wolves. A small population might exist for, say, fifty years. But we should not confuse existence with persistence."

Curiously, the 1893 wolf displayed at the Adirondack Museum played a pivotal role in the persistence/existence question. Mitochondrial DNA analysis conducted by Paul Wilson in the wildlife forensic laboratory at Ontario's Trent University indicates that coyote-related DNA, not gray wolf, was present in a tiny sample of hide from that specimen. This evidence led to serious questions about whether a new canid population would remain racially pure.

The eighty-four-page report, commissioned by the Defenders of Wildlife, cost the organization $114,000. Conducted by the Oregon-based Conservation Biology Institute, the study was completed in October and scheduled to be unveiled in early December. The press conference was delayed, but the news that gray wolves weren't right for the park after all was just too juicy to stay under wraps. By the time the advisory committee meeting was held in Saranac Lake, the canid was out of the bag and into the newspapers.

It was an odd session. Committee members—representing farmers, hunters, hikers, guides, biologists and preservationists—were cordial, but media associates were cranky. If this was a news conference, where was the news? The situation was made more awkward by the eager questions from the audience who wished for answers from scientists who wrote the report—who weren't present. Copies of the study were distributed (you can read it online at www.consbio.org), and folks drifted off into the night.

Actually, another aspect of the committee's work was supposed to be released at that time: the preliminary assessment of social feasibility by Jody Enck and Tommy Brown, of Cornell University. In a nutshell, it looks like the 422 Adirondackers they interviewed were lukewarm to the notion of gray wolves in their wilderness. Seventeen percent neither approved nor disapproved; the remainder were split down the middle. Not exactly a resounding mandate. Statewide, sixty percent of the 500 people surveyed favored reintroduction, thirty-four percent were indifferent and six percent were opposed. However, the report's introduction cautioned, "the proportion of residents who hold either positive or negative attitudes about restoration should never be used as a surrogate referendum." I understand that it is important to know the reasons people feel the way they do, but why then ask for thumbs up or thumbs down?

The next day, with dogged tenacity, Defenders of Wildlife issued a press release indicating the group was "disappointed in the report's conclusions." On the heels of that, Defenders president Rodger Schlickeisen said, "Our biggest regional question now is which wolf should we be planning for? If the Canadian genetics study holds up to peer review, the Adirondacks ... may turn out to be the long-sought home for a second population of red wolves in the United States." The statement didn't get much local play, but I distinctly heard howls of protest.

—MARCH/APRIL 2000

Shake a Tail Feather
Watching an unlikely lord of the dance

WHEN, EXACTLY, DOES spring begin in the Adirondacks? Most of us could agree on the arrival of winter's first breathtaking blast, but its end is another story. The next season wobbles forward in trepid fits, unconvinced of its own inevitability and easily trounced into chill submission by another cold snap, another dump of snow. Spring waffles just when we want proof.

Longer days confirm our hopeful suspicions; we're forced to study the heavens and Earth for signs, scanning the skies for a skein of geese, divining the dirt for a morsel of color other than brown, gray or white. Our visual focus is razor sharp, when maybe we ought to trust our ears instead. The hills are alive with the sounds of sex.

It's a complex composition—as elaborately woven as threads of DNA—part symphony, part hoedown, with touches of avant-garde ballet, Broadway blockbuster and Gregorian chant. There's plenty of percussion: the thrum of the partridge, drumming his wings for all he's worth as he poses heroically on a stump. And woodwinds: tree frogs trill from the branches; bullfrogs bellow in the shallows. These are minor players, though, as spring's curtain rises.

Consider the American woodcock as potential star of the

season: he sings and dances. No-necked, bug-eyed, mulch-colored, short-legged, long-nosed, this round mound of ground-bound fowl looks like something cobbled out of leftover parts from nature's homely storehouse. A common North Country bird for eight or nine months of the year, it spends most of its life hunkered down on the forest floor, blending in with dead leaves, probing for earthworms with a long, almost prehensile beak. (The top mandible can actually flex to extract a nightcrawler from the mud.) If you were to pick a creature—based on eye appeal—this bird lurks at the bottom of the studmuffin list. Bright-hued songbirds or fleet-winged raptors could be top contenders; this nondescript ball would surely be the nadir.

Think again. The male woodcock is a dancing fool with more moves than Baryshnikov. He's a virtuoso musician too: call him Bobby McPheromone for all the strange sounds emanating from unbridled lust. The guy is not shy when his mojo is working. The 1903 book *Bird Life* puts it this way: "As a songster the woodcock is unique among our summer birds. Ordinarily sedate and dignified, even pompous in his demeanor, in the spring he falls a victim to the passion which is accountable for so many strange customs in the bird world."

In late April and May open fields throughout the North Country set the stage for the woodcock premiere. Don't worry about watching; the birds couldn't care less about your presence. (And, possiblly, they're responsible for the phrase "snipe hunting" entering our language.) At dusk listen for a buzzy, nasal, insistent, electronic "*Beent! Beent!*" Then countdown: ten, nine, eight ... liftoff! Mr. Woodcock rockets—sort of—from the ground, aerodynamic as a water balloon sent skyward by slingshot. Clumsy-quick like a bat, he circles wide, wings voicing an eerie, bubbling twitter. He ascends higher, circles tighter, fluttering, twittering, then vanishing into the black sky. Once he's up 200 or 300 feet—reduced to sound and sensed motion, formless—he's silent. Then he zigzags to the ground, chirping, to the spot where it all began. Pause. Then "*Beent! Beent!*" and we're off again.

The extravagant mating display can last half an hour or more on a spring evening; on full-moon nights the show may go until dawn. The dance has two purposes: to warn other swains to stay away and to attract a bride. A male's territory can be studio-apartment size—a hundred square feet of flat ground—or a country estate spanning a couple of acres. A prime field, edged by mucky woods for good worm hunting, may be the theater for several bachelors stomping up a storm.

Females watch from the sidelines, and when one spots an appealing fellow, she steps forward to his territory. They gurgle softly to each other, then *Beent*! together. At this point, the human observer goes from spectator to voyeur. Usually it's too dark to see what happens next—he rushes at her, wings raised. One ancient bird book dryly notes that male woodcocks are "believed to be promiscuous." That's understandable: considering how much effort goes into the exhibition, why stop dancing when there may be more mates in wait? Male woodcocks remain bachelors forever, unconcerned with the mundane chores of family life.

After that brief encounter, the lady woodcock's work begins. On the edge of the parade ground, fairly out in the open, she scuffs the ground a bit and tosses in some leaves and dry grass. There she lays four eggs and incubates them, listening to the serenade. After three weeks, her brood hatches into precocious puffballs—among them an understudy or two, primed to learn the ancient steps.

—MAY/JUNE 2000

Freezing Points
Are we headed for Adirondack winter lite?

"WINTER LIES TOO long in country towns, hangs on until it is stale and shabby, old and sullen." While I have no quarrel with Willa Cather's observation, it appears to me that our dreaded North Country winters are incrementally losing their grim, grinding power. Not that winter doesn't still possess the ability to catch us utterly unprepared with freak combinations of cold, wind, rain, snow, thunder, lightning, ice, warm and everything but frozen frogs falling from the sky. Still, at the risk of annoying the weather makers, doesn't it seem that we're enjoying Adirondack Winter Lite as the twenty-first century dawns?

Maybe it's the cloudy lens of memory that holds up winters past as the true trials of our hardy spirits. Maybe it's the contrast between times when the snow settled in serenely on Thanksgiving and ebbed away at Easter, and recent days, when fickleness rules: Januaries with shirt-sleeve temperatures launching monsoon downpours causing basement-pumping marathons. One January thaw is to be expected, makes a nice break you might say, but three—as happened in 1995, with each punctuated by frigid flooding—is a bit much. And no one who lived through it will forget the ice storm of 1998.

Old-fashioned winters were like plodding oxen, dragging cold down from the north, unfurling a counterpane of pristine white behind them. My first cold season in the North Country was 1976–1977; snow seemed to fall in feathery six- to eight-inch blankets every night. We lived near the end of a long road, the other inhabitants being the man with the snowplow and his wife. We barely saw him, as the banks grew taller, and waited for him to clear a trail before we headed off to start our days in the world beyond our socked-in woods.

That winter I was formally introduced to the wonderful insulating properties of snow and heard trees crack like rifle shots and the ice *ba-boom* like a kettledrum. I had my first (and second and third) taste of the manifold joys of roof shoveling. (Let the record state that Wisconsin, where I grew up, has ample snow and cold. I just don't recall winter being so elongated that spring was compressed into half an hour on a late April morning.) We gave up shoveling the roof when there was no place for the snow to go; the heaps on the ground went up to the eaves. This made it easy, of course, to get down off the housetop—toss the tools and leap. I never pictured, though, that I'd be peering out of windows that allowed only a narrow band of view above their static white horizon. Watching voles and mice tunnel through snow smack against the panes turned those same windows into giant ant farms.

That prodigiously precipitated season was not embroidered by my mind's eye; it was snowy to the extreme. Official records from the central Adirondacks show that sixty-seven inches of snow fell in November, sixty-three in December, ninety-five in January, seventy-six in February and sixty-three in March. (Statistics for April are curiously absent, no doubt because the recorder either was fully buried or had summarily fled to a more salubrious clime, like Buffalo.) That adds up to thirty feet of snow. Of course, the stuff compacted and melted and generally reduced itself over time, but it does explain the need to shovel. A lot. It also explains why our dogs went into full-blown cabin fever, contenting themselves in our absence with such waggish games as Put the Tennis Ball Under the Couch and Bark Till

Someone Comes to the Door, Shred the Shower Curtain to Shrapnel and Let's Run Up and Down the Hallway with the Toilet Paper Twirling As the Roll Disappears.

Then there was cold. Not that winter in particular, and not dinky snaps and wee spells, but solid weeks of subzero—tedious, droning agony, like a dull toothache. February 1979 springs to mind as a month of yore, exactly one year before Lake Placid's Winter Olympics, when preparations were in frenzied overdrive. That is, until Saturday the tenth dawned, and things ground to a halt. The mercury went on strike, stubbornly refusing to migrate upward of minus thirty-five or dip below minus forty-two. These distinctions are abstract in the extreme; you get an ice-cream headache regardless, and when the car won't start on the first day of thirty below, the situation is not going to change over the next six days of same.

The episode brings to mind Robert Louis Stevenson's recollection of wintering in Saranac Lake, 1887–1888: "You should see our back log when the thermometer goes (as it does go) away—away below zero, till it can be seen no more by the eye of man—not the thermometer, which is still perfectly visible, but the mercury which curls up in the bulb like a hibernating bear." A few months later, RLS commented, "It is odd, zero is like summer heat to us now."

That was then, this is now. Forecasters can say what they will about a long and strong or short and sweet winter to come, but I'll let somebody cross the lake ice first.

—JANUARY/FEBRUARY 2001

Blinded by the Light
Cultivating the senses of place

LIGHT HAS REMARKABLE, changeable qualities in the Adirondacks. In winter it can be pink, floating warmth over a chill landscape, or blue, tinting a blank canvas of snow to mirror an austere sky. In summer, light has depth and heft to it, a physical intensity that bears down like gravity or hauls a scene right into the viewer's eyes and brain.

The best summer days are those glowing ones, when all disheveled nature stands out in brilliant gilt-edged isolation, when the longest, widest vistas are as blowtorch sharp as the silver-burnished blueberries at your feet. The scales of a red pine tree aren't merely brown in this light, they're umber, rust and raw sienna in distinct oblong plaques, with deep greenish-black edges where they overlap. Or study the delirious color scheme of red-osier dogwood; out of the ground rises a clump of shiny, smooth, slender canes, with lime-green bark that segues to yellow-orange, red and finally deep maroon. Comprehend for a moment that the vermilion edge outlining a painted turtle's shell is close to the color of cardinal flower petals that ring the turtle's pond or the back of a scarlet tanager as he darts away from the same water's emerald border. Coincidence? Or reward for attending to detail? Think about the water of a favorite trout stream; the same gin-clear liquid that spills over your fingers transforms to weak tea, nut-brown ale and finally stout, complete with foamy head. Light connects, light separates.

There's more than color to Adirondack vision on one of these days, there's the orderly perspective of a chosen landscape, the way lumpy mountains pile up on each other, chaos at first sight, then foreground, midground, background, sky. The topography emerges so that we can build a mind map, plot that yes, this peak is before that one, or yes, that pond is nestled between those two hills. Imagine that view with the eyes of a dragonfly, each orb with 50,000 facets, each dragonfly brain capable of processing a hundred hues to every nuance we pride ourselves on seeing. Try those mountains from a peregrine's point of view, winging a hundred miles an hour above the highest trees—yet able to spot a chickadee darting past the forest margin. Vision must be true and trustworthy for that predator to succeed.

Sight is, of course, the prideful sense, the arrogant sense, and it's only fitting for humans to be so dependent on it. Seeing is believing. It's why we value eyewitness accounts. It's how we prove something to be so. But vision is a quick picture. Light travels too fast.

When it comes to the other senses, we're babes in the woods; our equipment is crude, our skills undeveloped. A barn owl can hear a mouse's footsteps and relies completely on sound to capture prey. Bats use sound not only to hunt but for navigation; sound distinguishes space from solid. These are specifics. Wild country is saturated with noise and song that humans are scarcely prepared to understand. The multitude of sounds in the woods contains as much meaning and complexity as a Mahler symphony, with bird notes filling in for oboe, flute, horn and percussion. I would love to stand in a clearing and hear the natural interplay with the same appreciation I have for music. I could learn, I suspect.

One thing that probably can't be learned, though, is to perceive scents like a dog. Smells exist in three dimensions for a beagle sniffing along a trail—up, down, over, under—but there's also the element of time. Scent is ephemeral on the wind, yet lingers on the ground for nose-driven beasts. This fragrance is fresh, from a bobcat marking his territory only hours before; this smell is older, a deer's bed of last night. These clues are important to a dog, historical information to be sifted out from the kinds of scent we notice: the must of rotting leaves, the haylike perfume of balsam, the tang of pine.

"Viewshed" is one of those twentieth-century words that has a certain usefulness but no real poetry. It describes a pristine vista that should not be defaced. Someday we may come to value wild country as sound garden or scent sanctuary, worthy of attention and respect.

—JULY/AUGUST 2001

The Blue Goose
Flyaway or victim of fowl play

ONE OCTOBER A few years back, an unexpected guest arrived at some lakeside cabins in Blue Mountain Lake. The place had shut down for the winter—pipes drained, beds stripped, curtains drawn—but that suited this transient just fine. All he needed was food, water and a place to rest.

The visitor was a snow goose, a surprising bird to appear on the ground in the central Adirondacks, although I've been lucky to glimpse one or two skeins as they've passed overhead. Snow geese are smaller and subtler than the rude Canadian honkers; their wings beat with a faint sound between a *whoosh* and a whistle. When their luminous white bodies sail against the fall sky it's like the passage of a flock of ghosts.

Snow geese nest on Canada's northernmost fringes, a narrow strip of territory from Hudson Bay to Coronation Gulf, and when they migrate south they fly all night and all day, stopping only when they spy a marshy area with plenty of grass. When the flock reaches such a place only the promise of good weather—clear skies, a following wind, warm temperatures and starry nights—sends the birds back into the air. The journey between summer home and southern waters is 3,000 miles or more; though the geese can fly fifty miles an hour, the trip still takes a long time. A pair of eighteen-inch-long wings surely gets tired of moving a six-pound body through the clouds.

Why this particular bird ended up landbound and alone (snow geese take gregariousness to extremes; some 40,000 appeared at Lake Champlain's Point au Roche two years ago) became clear after a day or two. Walking was a problem; one foot flopped inward whenever he stood up. The bird could fly a little, although when people approached, hissing and looking ticked off were effective in keeping them a respectful distance away.

For a couple of weeks, at any town gathering, the stranded goose was a conversation given. Forget juicy gossip; the bird was the word. His behavior was minutely observed; theories were developed about the cause of his disabilities; proposals were made for a rescue. We had all heard stories about geese stuck in rapidly freezing ponds, and this guy needed to get up and get out. The time had come for action, not talk. But what sort of action?

The bird mustered an amazingly compassionate response. A bewildering array of food was left on the lawn—slices of bread and scoops of bird seed the most obvious because they remained untouched and possibly did more to attract prowling scroungers like coyotes than the presence of a plump, solitary, stationary fowl. Snow geese love to eat grass, which became patently clear after a few days, and their serrated beaks are adept at ripping up choice greens. They're so effective in grazing that they've destroyed their own arctic habitat, leaving cratered, sterile tundra in their wake. "Geese eat everything in front of them and mess everything behind them"—one of those old farmers' sayings—is true.

As the days got shorter and nastier the goose faction increased pressure for an intervention. Those who felt the situation would reach a natural resolution (fox fare or recovery given the tincture of time) kept their thoughts to themselves. The forest ranger got plenty of calls, but search and rescue for hapless humans, not animals, keeps him busy. The conservation officer likewise got calls and offers of help in capturing the fugitive. But attempts to get the goose in a net and away for rehabilitation were thwarted. The bird may have been used to seeing people at close range, but even a profound handicap didn't trump the wild urge to stay free.

Cold winds blew. The lawn dwindled. The bird stayed. A typical snow goose day was hunkering, eating, waddling, eating and enriching the soil, punctuated by a visit from meals on wheels. Then one morning, no goose. No scattering of feathers, no sign of struggle, just a wholesale departure as puzzling as his arrival.

Not knowing how the story ends isn't a bad thing. If the one-time goose of Blue found his way to some South Carolina slough, that's fine; if he fattened a fisher for the coming winter that's just as important.

—SEPTEMBER/OCTOBER 2001

The Color of Water
From fluid state to frozen in time

I LIVE BETWEEN two lakes, not twins at all or even distantly related. In fact, the watershed divide between the Hudson and the St. Lawrence may be right outside my living room. Lake Durant, shallow and man-made for log drives, flows south to the Hudson, its waters tumbling down the Rock and Cedar Rivers before joining the great one. Durant is overlooked, cars flying by on the state highway, and it hides its charms—sloughs, coves and miniature rocky cliffs—shyly. When the time comes for Durant to lock up and move into solid state, it does so peacefully, the skim of ice appearing one morning like a taut sheet of Saran Wrap. The bays fill in, then the main arm of the lake, in a couple of days.

In late fall Lake Durant, with its weeds and cranberry boglets, is a shuttle stop for waterfowl, not just drab black ducks and those overbearing Canada honkers, but bright tiny teal, elegant widgeons, maroon-headed ring-necked ducks and, once, a trio of swans. My neighbors regarded them as visiting royalty, and they usually responded in kind: graceful, aloof, dignified, floating serenely with ballerina poise. I watched through binoculars one afternoon from a tag-alder bank and was witness to all three dabbling in unison, their huge white butts pointed heavenward. So much for the regal imagery. A bird's got to eat sometime.

Blue Mountain Lake, its waters northbound and self-important, fusses and fumes over the inevitable freeze. It sulks and broods, becoming bluer and bluer, no longer obligated to reflect winter sky. The waves turn to lapis, labradorite, then ultramarine (the perfect name for that hue in that place), and this signals the next step. The free-form lake takes skim ice in its remote sheltered reaches. The rest of the waterway, buffeted by winds that hit the mountain and coil back, churns sluggishly. The islands grow pearly skirts. The shore shelves out inch by inch. Then one still day in late December the transformation is complete. The surface is pewter and hard as iron.

This marks a change in how we use the lake, not just how we observe its moods. The water is now the village green, accessible without boat or bathing suit. We can step off the town beach and stroll for miles, that is, of course, once the ice has thickened. The appeal of a large, flat, open, public space in a well-treed mountain town cannot be denied. I like to wait for New Year's Day, more to note the event than out of simple precaution. (I also like to see someone's tracks before I venture out.)

Some weekends the ice sheet draws all kinds of sports activity, from cross-country skiers towing kids on sleds to snowmobilers to ice fishermen. The frosty field is surprisingly popular for this contemplative pursuit, with clusters of tip-ups dotting the in-town bay. Only a few shanties appear; many anglers come only for a day. I have seen their catches, lake trout as long and big around as my leg, and marveled at how such a huge, ungainly creature squeezes through a hole in the ice that can't be much bigger than the hubcap on a coaster-wagon wheel.

I received ice-fishing gear for my birthday, and the pastime fits my level of patience, or my ability to be captivated by minutiae. However, I am usually on the ice in the company of dogs, not necessarily a good thing, what with hooks, minnows and hair-trigger flags on little sticks.

One clever beast of ours discovered he could flip a flag with a poke of his nose. From that moment, no well-set tip-up within shouting distance was safe. He would launch himself at a dead run, then weave and twist through the minefield of holes, orange squares popping up in his wake. One day he forced fishing parties to reset about two dozen rigs. The joke wore off quickly, and we avoided the best fishing spots for the duration of that season.

The lake is a gathering spot on starry nights, to look at the midnight-blue canopy pocked with planets and stars, the Milky Way slashing overhead, a diamond dusted creek. On those nights, the ice reverberates with solemn moans, part didgeridoo, part timpani, stirring and shuddering underfoot. Walking home on land, we can still hear the lake talking, and we fall asleep to its peculiar *baaooooms* and whale songs. Blue Mountain Lake is a living thing, and this ancient dialog cannot be obscured—if we choose to hear it.

—JANUARY/FEBRUARY 2003

That Sinking Feeling
Testing the waters in the merry month of May

THE SLIM WRAITH gestured away from shore, its lavender lips forming words lost in chattering teeth. I leaned closer to the milky pale figure, catching a clammy sensation from sheer proximity but not touch. "J-j-j-ust r-r-r-un and j-j-j-j-ump in!"

This is how Adirondack children dupe adults into swimming in May. Every spring, only a month or two after the ice goes out, the siren song of open waters beckons those without body fat or common sense. People above the age of consent would do well to resist, to hang back in the comfortable embrace of a beach chair while youngsters dash into frigid waves. But many grownups go bravely forward, only to think, I'll wait till the Fourth of July next year.

I am a deliberate swimmer. I don't need a bracing dip to count coup on the calendar. I grew up near Lake Michigan, which was rarely warm or welcoming. Mothers and babysitters alike presented the lake as perilous: schools of dead alewives, shards of broken glass and the mysterious undertow would make careless children sick, bloody or even drag them out beyond the lifeguard's reach. These admonishments stuck with me. I know what cold water is and don't require an annual baptism to remind me.

Messing about in boats is another matter. Blue Mountain Lake is so glorious as soon as it sheds its rigid carapace that water play in early spring is a necessary rite. The first canoe strokes cinch the new season in ways that lawn mowing or storm window removal do not. On one of these inaugural paddles many Mays ago, we discovered that two people, one large dog and simultaneously executed bow pry and stern draw equaled an abrupt turn, although not the smooth pivot we had in mind. The canoe rotated, you bet, from right-side-up to otherwise, in water the temperature of refrigerated soda. Luckily there was an island nearby; luckily, the dog suddenly recalled generations of retrievers before him and fetched all our floating gear.

You'd think we'd learn. A fine summer and fall of blissfully benign water smudged that memory into a comical footnote. The next Memorial Day weekend, with gentle breezes and a critical mass of hungry blackflies, sent us down to the lake again. This time our craft was a friend's sailboat, a tunnel-hulled scow that seemed more seaworthy than a Sunfish, more challenging, more capacious, more speedy. We set out, smug in our rudder handling. The day was full of promise, the lake virtually empty of other fun seekers.

The boat slowly questioned our commands. It wallowed. It hesitated. It failed to come about. The water, which had been a foot below the deck, got closer. Then the hull submarined. We came to the same lightning-fast epiphany: we were sinking. We had no choice, head for the nearest land, dragging the tub behind us.

The swimming was breathtaking enough, but towing the waterlogged boat was almost Sisyphean. For each forward inch there was a centimeter back. Thankfully, we weren't hugely far from landfall.

On the deserted island we moved around to get warm. A neighbor passed us on his party barge. We waved and yelled. He waved and yelled back, not realizing we were hollering

"Help!" rather than a friendly hello. After what felt like hours but must have been minutes, the friend who had loaned us the thing saw her craft was perched oddly among some rocks.

She paddled out in her kayak, assessed the situation and headed homeward to get her family's motorboat. Our rescue seemed assured. She arrived and we all began tying the sailboat to the water-ski line for the tow back to the dock. The motor sputtered and died. She pulled the cord, and the outboard roared to life. However, the boat did not move, or at least not forward. It began to drift away, much to the consternation of the captain.

The propeller had fallen off. I would like to say we saw its glinting descent into the deeps, and that we noticed the sailboat's drain plug was conspicuous in its absence, but the gravity of the situation had sapped our powers of observation. For the second time in one day we were stuck on an island with a disabled boat.

The afternoon was moving onward. We were not. After scanning the territory for would-be saviors, we accepted the fact that every other boater had gone home. There was one solution that came to mind—swim for shore. I was already freezing, not up to the task, and once again, the friend who had involved all of her fleet without having any fun in them, lit out for port, swimming strongly. Within half an hour we were toweling off in front of her fireplace. Half an hour after that we walked into the town diner in hopes of steaming coffee and soup.

Word of our adventure had reached the mainland before we did. As we approached the crowded counter, all heads swiveled in unison. "How's the water?"

—MAY/JUNE 2003

Gold Rush
The tamarack stars in fall's second act

A FALL TWO years ago is the one I remember best, the thrown stone in a river of memory, with ripples circling out to this day. The sky was Prussian blue, painfully vivid, with strands of geese unraveling on their southward flight, dozens, scores, then hundreds of them, their rhythmic squawking like the sound of unoiled oarlocks. From opaque cold water to clear sky, a connection.

Along the roads asters in white, lavender, rose and purple strained toward the sun, then turned to fuzzy tufts of wind-scattered seeds. The tiny leaves of wild strawberries scrawled bright scarlet against the sand. Rugosa roses, profligate in their thorns and persistent in their march across cleared land, achieved another sort of beautiful emphasis, the peach-colored hips swelling like crab-apples. At dusk, the crickets dwindled from a broken-record chorus to silence, and morning birdsong, a deafeningly insistent cacophony at four a.m. in the spring, became isolated to late risers, mobs of jays picking through the compost and departing loons wailing as they arced like arrows overhead. The scent of autumn was subtle, not the sharp dry tang of pine released by heat, but damp, ferny and organic, like a freshly turned garden. Brushing past gray birch yielded wintergreen wafts, and crushing tamarack needles brought a blend of grass, mint and cedar.

On the edge of my field the forest posed a jumble of intensity, blood red, sunflower yellow, pumpkin orange. Behind the showoffs, the hemlock, spruce and balsam stood, patient and green, waiting for what comes next. The hardwoods were nervous in a wind, their leaves flipping and rustling, and finally drifting to the ground.

The encore to that display waited in certain bogs, away from the head-turning mountainsides, where stands of tamarack shifted from sage to golden, fluffy and dignified at once. This tree is a contradiction, a deciduous conifer, an evergreen that mocks its classification. (All conifers lose their needles, but piecemeal, never doing a complete striptease.) The tow-headed tamarack has its moment in the grand progress of the season, before bare branches dominate the skyline. On the edges of overlooked wastelands it glows with singular intensity.

The tamarack never made an impact in Adirondack forestry. In the eighteenth century, wood from hackmatack (like larch, another name for *Larix laricina*) was praised for its strength and sought for ship timbers in Europe and the colonies, though it was not logged extensively in New York. Early guideboats may have used tamarack for rib stock, but spruce proved more plentiful, especially all those stumps and curved roots left behind by the armies of sawyers stripping the north woods for pulp. The dense, slow-to-rot tamarack lumber had local uses, things like fence posts and railroad ties; unfortunately, the wood also has a tendency to warp, making untrustworthy building components. Adirondack rivers never filled with tamarack during the spring log drives; it doesn't float very well.

Big tamaracks stretch to sixty feet high and tend to cluster in damp spots inhospitable to other species. Large stands of tamarack are rare; they're not that kind of tree. Larches are found from Quebec to the Midwest, but this uncommon tree is bound to become scarcer still.

Since the 1880s a tiny caterpillar from Europe has gradually destroyed full-grown tamaracks across their North American range. The larch casebearer hatches in the spring, a minute wriggler that bores into tamarack leaves, hollowing out the tissue. One casebearer (named for its cocoon, a gray-brown pellet about a quarter-inch long) eats dozens of needles in its march toward mothhood, and when hundreds of them inhabit a tree the outcome is often slow death.

Look closely at any Adirondack tree and you'll find some tiny organism designed to bring it down. Sugar maples have thrips; beetles, borers and blights all prey on specific forest dwellers. Some of the pests have been here all along, taking trees slowly without upsetting the woodland balance. Others are transplants, imported on lumber, plants or creeping toward our woods from the south. This painful truth doesn't offer a solution, since eradicating the insects on a widespread scale creates new problems.

Health is never guaranteed for any living thing, and even the largest and strongest become victims. Each season also brings the seeds of its own demise, the planned obsolescence that makes new growth possible. In November we can watch, wait and take stock of the world around us, laid bare by the coming cold.

—NOVEMBER/DECEMBER 2003

The Drifters
Floating the Hudson's heady waters

THERE'S SOMETHING ABOUT a river trip, the lure of pointing a boat downstream and coming out someplace else, becoming maybe somebody else in the process. Think of Huck Finn or Lewis and Clark. Lake travel tends to be circular, returning to the point of origin, but streamwork has a different feel. There's a clear destination, with details unfolding en route, like a good book, with plot, characters, setting and dialogue. Any good river talks to people, muttering, mumbling, chattering, shouting.

Our thirty-mile float trip down the Hudson from Newcomb to North River had to happen in a narrow window: the water had to be high enough to make easy passage in the northern stretches, which turn into boulder gardens in summer, and low enough that the gorge itself, seventeen miles of white water, isn't as steep as a black-diamond ski run. Of course that coincides with prime time for bugs. Overnighting in the backcountry in June needs a good explanation.

My husband, Tom, and I had always been curious about the river around Newcomb, the sinuous flow near Tahawus—whose shoreline is now for sale—that was once harnessed to crush ore and run blast furnaces. We had also heard about Ord Falls and

Blackwell Stillwater from an Indian Laker who had gone south with the last log drives. We knew about a cross carved high in a pine memorializing a lumberjack who never made it home one spring. We wanted to be there, to catch the storied stream.

But it's the impossible dream for flat-water, open-canoe paddlers. Call it our own Adirondack river of no return. The twelve miles from the Route 28N bridge in Newcomb to the Cedar River is simply beautiful and beautifully simple, with only a handful of camps, one bridge and a dirt road or two to break the untouched feel. The problem lies in the commitment required once you put in: There's no public exit before you reach the gorge, which spits, foams and churns from Class III to V. The northern half is bucolic, lazy rafting with some spunky ripples to keep you alert. If the passage could be an out-and-back route (tough because of the current) or if there were a public take-out after ten or fourteen miles, this would be among the most popular day trips in the park. Reality is the trek requires a guide with the right kind of rig or excellent paddling skills in a decked white-water canoe or downriver kayak.

Only a few outfitters offer this expedition, partly because the timing is so critical. We booked our trip with Beaver Brook Outfitters, based in Wevertown and known for expert fishing and rafting guides. But we delayed our launch, lollygagged for a couple of years. The weather didn't cooperate. When the water level was ideal it snowed, or the river fell so fast we'd have to work extra hard to keep moving. Finally we picked a date, the first weekend in June, and figured rain wouldn't hurt us, it couldn't be that cold and the trout fishing might be great.

We lucked out, scoring a river running just over five feet, fine for taking an inflatable boat with a rowing rig through the gorge and nice for the slower sections. Temperatures were in the sixties, with blue sky and a breeze of maybe five miles an hour to baffle the bugs. Happily, we were the only sports with Pete Burns, a twenty-four-year-veteran guide, so we could bring a mountain of gear if we wanted to fly-fish, spincast, troll, shoot pictures, eat real food, carry thick sleeping-bag pads and bring all the creature comforts.

An array of coolers, duffels, stuff sacks, even a table that rolled up into a bag with four screw-in legs fit nicely into the Aire raft, a fourteen-footer with a tubular metal frame to support oarlocks and seats fore and aft plus a bench for the rower in the middle. I sat figurehead in the bow when we launched, in a perch with nothing but water beneath me. It was unnerving, having no sense of the boat behind and nothing but river in front. For the nine hours we were on the river and the night we camped we saw no one else. This kind of solitude is rare, even in the Adirondacks.

We fished in pools, dropped wet flies and nymphs in riffles, watched the forest unspool. A kingfisher traced our route, then swooped away. Chickadees called to each other from one bank to the other. We drifted, talked and spun through Class III water—our own amusement park teacup ride. The current did a lot of the work; our job was to take it all in. The guide's job was to make it all feel effortless, with undisguised joy at being on his home turf on a fine day.

We didn't spot much wildlife. What seemed to be a mink crossing bravely turned out to be a bedraggled chipmunk who had washed through some rough rapids. We scooped him with a net and deposited him in a sunny spot on the mainland. Why did the chipmunk cross the river was our joke for about a mile, then another striped swimmer shot across our bow. This guy was doing fine, clearly on a mission with the muscle to carry it out. Were the chipmunks separated, like kids at girls' and boys' camps? Or do chipmunks get that old lemming urge to discover what lies ahead?

The fishing was casual. Tom got a strike and then whatever was on the hook played possum. He reeled in, only to find an odd silver fish about a foot long that came to furious thrashing life in the bottom of the raft. Fallfish, our guide said, not for keeping. We caught three more of these giant creek chubs, but no trout. No big deal.

Our campsite, a bench where the Cedar enters the Hudson, was surrounded by the chatter of fast water. The spot was clean, no detritus like you might find at picnic or tent sites in the gorge. Burns told us this was a favorite river drive stop, that the loggers working for Finch, Pruyn & Company slept under big felt blankets from the paper machines, six or more under a thick mat. Cozy, I'm sure. Tom and I had a tent, Burns had his, and in between were our kitchen and family room. Dinner was barbecued chicken, corn on the cob, salad, with strawberry shortcake for dessert.

We awakened early to about thirty degrees, puffs of fog accenting every groggy statement. We got food in our bellies, cleaned up camp and loaded the boat in record time. Holding a mug of coffee only warms so much of a body. Besides, the big river was up, and we weren't sure there'd be a dam release on the Indian River. The water level was fine, but more volume would make the rapids snappy to say the least. No fishing unless we eddied out, and then it would have to be with a well-placed fly.

We launched, our stuff stowed more carefully, our attention always ahead. The day was blue and clear, with tack-sharp light making monster shadows. What had seemed so benign the day before became serious terrain, steep rock banks, big boulders in the stream and then the sound—a drone of primal thunder held in by the canyon walls. I opted for the backseat, weighing my odds of falling into the boat rather than completely out of it.

Burns just smiled and pulled and pushed on the oars. In this boat, the rower faces downstream and steers with ten-foot oars, sweeping and ruddering. We hit a few bumps and the fun began. Twists, turns, drops. Facefuls of water. Ferry across. Find a V through slick smooth water. Burns grinned. The boat went as if by telepathy. This was beyond reading the water; it was from years of living the Hudson's nuances and power. We eddied out, splashed but spirits undampened. Burns laughed. In fact, he'd been chuckling the entire time. Tom took the oars.

Corklike we continued through big water, sideways down a few cascades, and only once stopped dead on a high ledge with water screaming around us. A real river rat would rattle off the rapids—Blue Ledge, Osprey Nest, Fox Den, Gunsight, Harris Rift—but as I tried to nail the names of these landmarks, I learned many of them have two or more titles. The river driver's Black Hole is now Bus Stop or Greyhound Bus, depending on whom you talk to; one person's Elephant Rock is another's Fish

Rock. Oh well. My favorite spot wasn't in the water, anyway; it was the Room of Doom, a crack cave in the eastern bank.

Tumbling and soaring for hours, our party encountered a couple of bigger rafts that had started with the bubble—the dam release from Lake Adirondack. Those folks were wearing wet suits and helmets, while we had our life vests and ordinary quick-dry clothing. We had comfort and style on our side, plus a raft that could turn on a dime with a nickel back and a tip of the hat from our guide.

The exuberant water eventually calmed to a steady, wide channel. We half-asked if we could run through the rapids paralleling Route 28, Perry's and the quick cascades closer to North Creek. But our ride to the outfitter's base was waiting. Hauling our boat and gear up the bank brought us swarms of blackflies and down to Earth. We were miles from where we started, and for a moment we were miles from who we had been a few days before, savoring the gift of fluid conversation and hours well spent on a liquid blue highway.

—2004 ANNUAL GUIDE TO THE GREAT OUTDOORS

Blood Sport
How I almost missed the Miracle on Ice

FROM THE TRAVELERS AID office in Saranac Lake we had a micro-macro perspective on the 1980 Winter Olympics, not quite inside the big snowy machine, but definitely more involved than the man on the street. We dealt with the hassles, not the disasters. We heard the radio chatter from the Red Cross and Olympic personnel and did what we could when the State Police called. Our contact with the competitions was limited to practices we could attend in spare moments away from the phones. We helped tourists who missed charter flights back to who-remembers-where, reunited groups that had split up in the course of wandering Lake Placid's Main Street, assisted in getting a few miscreants out of the country, arranged train, plane and automobile connections for the clueless. It was twenty-four hours on, twenty-four off, the days smearing like so many slushy sidewalks. Headquarters were above a bar, so we could lower a basket down an old laundry chute, with a note requesting a burger and a Coke. Night after night. Eric Heiden's pumping thirty-two-inch thighs, flying East German bobsleds, sailing ski jumpers—those images were for the paying customers. The events belonged to them, not us.

Except for one. A block of hockey tickets had been reserved

for New York State legislators, and we knew the late-afternoon game would include the U.S., maybe the Czechs, maybe the Finns, maybe the Soviet Union. The pols weren't biting, so my coworker and I snagged three tickets, one for each of us plus my boyfriend. The seats were prime, fourth row behind a goal. Then word came that the game would be our guys against the Soviets: bigger, stronger, bears on skates. Those hand-me-down tickets suddenly became a hot commodity. Fine. We weren't about to miss what appeared to be a pivotal skirmish in the Cold War.

Standing in line in the arena, it was close quarters, and the crowd snaked up the stairs, shuffling tiny steps in oversize boots. Three burly fellows, dressed in a zoo's worth of pelts, were mumbling away in Russian directly in front of us. Then jabber turned to jab—*YOW*! I got a very solid elbow in the nose from Mr. Minsk. Direct hit! Suddenly I had a twin-nostril gusher, and stars twinkled overhead. Mr. Pinsk and Mr. Murmansk muttered on, unaware of the impact.

We tried to stanch the flood. Big red rose petals bounced off the concrete. As nosebleeds go, this was epic epistasis. People around us didn't seem to notice, and we were stuck in line, dripping away. My face was a mess. When we got to the top of the stairs a state trooper spotted me, and we finally got free of the crush. "You need help?" he asked.

"I'm heading for our seats," my optimistic partner said, "You have your ticket, right?"

The trooper and I navigated the labyrinth leading to the first-aid cubicle, where a doctor and nurse cleaned up my combat face. They checked my pupils and pulse. They dabbed at me with peroxide-soaked gauze. They looked up my nose and clucked. The doctor thought I should go to the hospital for packing, and I insisted no way was I missing the game. So with a bag of ice, wadding under my upper lip and a slight dent in my courage, I tried to find the way back to the arena.

I could smell the crowd, all that wet wool, and hear the rumble of thousands of fans. But I couldn't find the door. I wandered down one corridor, only to be met by the tallest cops I've ever seen. They loomed over me. "Where do you think you're going?" reverberated down the cavernous corridor. "Where have you been?" was a better question, since I was far, far away from any public entrance.

I lost it. I blubbered something like "A Russian hit me ... *sniff, gulp* ... I want to see the game. I can't go to the hospital!" For some reason this performance was convincing and when my partner and coworker looked up, there I appeared, with my Goliath escort of guys in gray. "You rate! Have a beer," said a spectator in the row behind us.

I hate team sports, except for hockey and polo, in which you must have other, more important skills to score. Hockey as skating is gorgeous to see, all that speed, swooping and abrupt stopping. Polo too, the pounding hooves, backspins, grace, power and the occasional full-body crash.

It was a calm game for me. I couldn't risk another trip to first aid, where they'd surely whisk me to an emergency room. But between the drama, goals, saves, goals, there was a happy serenity to the event. When the first period ended and the refs were twirling around the rink, a Frisbee appeared. A striper caught it deftly. He flipped it into the stands. The crowd roared. The disk returned to the ice, and the ref got it, with more enthusiasm this time. He faked left. The crowd roared again. He faked right. More noise, then the disk sailed up to some troopers on a high tier. They tossed it back down. More shouts, more disk play. Then the teams poured onto the rink and the second period began. Pandemonium.

The concessionaires, with their heavy trays of beer, decided this one night that the spirit of international brotherhood would prevail over the capitalist ethic. One sat in the aisle next to us and gave away all his beer. He stayed for the rest of the game.

The second period ended, and the Frisbee reappeared. The sound was deafening, as sections of seats vied for the officials' tosses. The Zamboni nearly got a standing ovation. The driver waved, tipping his hat, to even greater approval. Clean ice has never been so publicly admired. As the teams emerged from the locker rooms, the roof shuddered from the racket. On the Richter scale, it was a quake felt round the planet.

When it was all over, 10,000 incredulous fans left that

charmed spot, and the party spilled onto the street. All over town people were standing on the rooftops, screaming; the sidewalks were thronged with the ecstatic. The vanquished vanished. The fur hats and coats blended into the dark night. Everybody knew, and the news traveled up and down Main Street, out onto Mirror Lake where Ingemar Stenmark was getting his slalom gold medal and the laser show lit up the sky. The word was a tsunami, carrying revelers into the Hilton, where sportscaster Jim McKay was dancing with an Olympic hostess. I swear trucks and cars were honking in Tupper Lake and we could hear them in Placid.

    The party went on and on, as did the hangovers. I can't recall the stick play at all, or the names of more than one or two U.S. players. But that feeling, of being among thousands of very happy people, that stays.

—JANUARY/FEBRUARY 2005

New Loon
How Adirondacks' favorite fowl went from vilified to glorified

BY MID-OCTOBER ADULT common loons are gone from the lakes, southbound to open water. But their young of last spring—homely as cormorants—linger, perfecting their wing skills and gaining strength for the migration. Parents and offspring are unlikely to meet ever again, one of the abiding mysteries of these birds. The few juveniles who survive from speckled egg to downy chick to gray-feathered swimmer are left to instinct and chance to find the saltwater home that will be theirs for three years, until they return to the Adirondacks in the black-and-white plumage we love so well.

There is another mystery surrounding these animals: Why do we care so deeply about a creature that can barely walk and has no use at all our world? This magnificent obsession is new to us, a product of the late twentieth century, when the birds became synonymous with wilderness. Loon imagery is rampant today, a cliché embroidered on golf shirts and hand towels, printed on doormats and gimme caps, embossed on brass plates, carved in stone and wood and cast in plastic. The streamlined torpedo shape and high-contrast paint job are so prevalent in decor and design that an outside observer—say, a desert dweller—would assume loons to be the requisite monogram for a happy home and a stylish wardrobe.

Loons in the twenty-first century have organizations dedicated to their survival, such as the North American Loon Fund and the Adirondack Cooperative Loon Project. Other beautiful birds, like kingfishers or herons or cedar waxwings, don't earn such partisan support; groups like Pheasants Forever and Ducks Unlimited have motives other than pure preservation for the game birds. Hunters love them, yes, and wish to conserve vital habitat, but the drive to increase populations is inseparable from the love of the chase. You can't shoot a loon today, nor would you want to eat one. But that wasn't always the case. These deep divers were targets, not of affection or respect, but prey sighted down the barrel of a nineteenth-century rifle.

You can hear the trigger click and smell the gunpowder in numerous accounts. "Loon-Shooting in a Thunderstorm," a stirring chapter in William H. H. Murray's 1869 best seller *Adventures in the Wilderness*, describes in detail a guide and sport firing merrily away at a frantic, evasive bird. Murray marvels, "Loons are the shyest and most expert swimmers of all waterfowl. Twenty rods is as near as you can get to them. When under fire, they sink themselves into the water so that nothing but the feathers along their backs and heads are in sight, and so quick are they that they dive at the flash, getting under in time to escape the bullet." Murray unloads so much lead that his gun overheats. The bird, stripped of back feathers from bullets, survives.

In an 1880 Vassar College alumni magazine, an anonymous young woman describes a loon hunt in Blue Mountain Lake. A professor staying at a hotel had challenged a local guide to bag him a bird to use as a taxidermy specimen, promising five dollars for the trouble, as much as two days' pay. A brace of boats race across the water, one with the hunter, the other trying to corral the bird. As the clouds lower and wind builds to a gale, the men row in crazy circles, firing repeatedly. At last all is quiet, so the author heads to the scene, observing, "When we came up to them, they had landed, and pulled the boat partially onto a rock. Behold! Our young man had not shot a loon, or a girl, or even Blue Mountain, but the boat."

Gavia immer 2, *Homo sapiens* 0. Many shooters thought they were correcting a new, terrible imbalance in nature. Trout were declining at an alarming rate in the Adirondacks as the 1800s came to a close, and publications such as the state fisheries and game reports kept that anti-loon sentiment alive in articles like "Winged Enemies of Fish" (1898). The northern diver, with its spear beak, "savage disposition" and arrow swiftness under water, was a prime suspect in the disappearance of speckled trout.

Killing the birds was entirely justified from a gamekeeper's perspective: "We do not see and therefore do not know the full extent of the depredations continually going on around us, but when we stop to realize the fruits of our labor and patient expectation, we are astonished by the scarcity of fish and often inclined to place the blame where it does not belong. Nature's checks upon overproduction are sometimes more effective than man's most ingenious devices for the legitimate capture or legal destruction of fish, but at the present state of the fishing waters in New York it is safe to say that we can get along without nature's checks." It was also safe to say that blasting a loon or two was regarded as a positive act, especially by hatchery managers and wildlife experts such as the author of "Winged Enemies." Though many states discussed placing a bounty on loons, it was never legislated in New York. There was no need to spend tax dollars encouraging something that was so popular on its own.

Glancing at old photographs showing gentlemen posing by clotheslines laden with fish ranging in size from trophies to tie tacks might make a modern observer think otherwise about the cause of the anglers' woes. As early as 1919 ornithologist A. C. Bent is catching on: "Even the lively trout, noted for its quickness of movement, cannot escape the loon, and large numbers of these desirable fish are destroyed to satisfy its hunger. Some sportsmen have advocated placing a bounty on loons on this account, but as both loon and trout have always flourished together until the advent of sportsmen, it is hardly fair to blame this bird, which is such an attractive feature of the wilds, for the scarcity of the trout. We are too apt to condemn a bird for what little damage it does in this right, without giving it credit for the right to live."

A few outdoorsmen began to notice a change in northern waters. "Loons are not as plentiful in the Adirondacks as they were five years ago," writes *Field and Stream*'s Adirondack columnist, Harry V. Radford, in 1901. "I do not hear their strange wild call in the silence of the night, or see them sitting motionless in the water or diving elusively at the flash of the rifle, as often as I used to, and I am sorry for it." He straddles a curious fence, admitting the birds' scarcity while indicating the reason for it. The $64,000 question: What does Radford miss more? The call of the wild or the crack of a rifle?

"It was asserted by the best authorities that this bird can evade a gunshot by diving at the flash, and I have no doubt that this is true when black powder is used, but when a modern smokeless rifle is discharged at a loon, he is utterly unable to dodge the shot, even when intently eyeing the gunner all the time," writes Elon Howard Eton in a New York State Museum bulletin published in 1910. In a scientific study the species is still noted mainly as an effective predator of fish. But this interpretation had recently come under fire.

Attitudes toward wilderness were changing across the country, and grudging admiration of birds and animals for their own sake became more common in the press. Bird-watching, as opposed to bird-shooting, was gaining popularity as a hobby. Conservation efforts, some launched by the brand-new Audubon Society, brought the carnage of the feather trade to widespread attention. *Birds of America*, first printed in 1917, admits, "The cry of the loon has been variously described as mournful, mirthful, sinister, defiant, uncanny, demoniacal and so on. At any rate, it is undeniably distinctive and characteristic and it is almost certain to challenge the dullest ear and the most inert imagination, while in those who instinctively know the voices of nature, especially when she is frankly and unrestrainedly natural, it produces a thrill and elicits a response which only the elect understand."

The elect—just who would they be? Not the guides who earned their pay tending to city men playing in the woods. That kind of assertion about a chosen group more inclined to observe nature as an adoring bystander points to growing class differences in appreciating the wild. The educated—with means, leisure and a lakefront camp—were likely to see loons as important symbols of the Adirondacks and the great untamed reaches of North America. As game laws were codified to protect stocks of deer and fish, the idea of preserving nature grew into a national consciousness. One concrete proof of this is the federal Migratory Bird Treaty Act of 1918, which banned possessing or killing hundreds of bird species as well as collecting their eggs, and transporting and trading skins and other parts. The law destroyed forever the commerce in wild feathers, so sought after for ladies' hats. The same people who could afford fancy millinery could also afford to save animals whose commercial worth was gone. The common loon, though rarely used in high fashion, benefited from the treaty. No longer could the great northern diver be regarded—legally—as a hunter's prize.

The broad reach of federal law enforcement was absent from North Country waters for decades following the bird protection act. Prohibition gave government agents plenty to do here anyway. The loon quietly slipped back into the shadows of its favorite bays, raising generations of chicks as the grand hotels slowly faded away. You can't miss something until it's gone. Or going. Loons began to vanish from former haunts, victims of so many human actions. The birds died from complications of acid rain, from ingesting lead shot and sinkers, from eating mercury-laden fish, from the subtle effects of shoreline development. Nests and eggs were destroyed by high water, sometimes the direct result of motorboat wakes. The birds' taste for lakefront is often similar to ours—a gentle slope to the water, not too many rocks, solitude. Vacation homes sent nesting pairs deeper into real wilderness, farther from sight. By the 1980s loon populations were watched with the same close scrutiny as the stock market. As the animals themselves disappeared, their value as symbols rose, just as interest in moose, wolf and other "charismatic megafauna" grew.

How we love to pretend we tread lightly on the land. How we yearn for simpler days and the perfection of untouched vistas. Loon lust is for a glance at a time when human activity was minimal, when creatures of the wind, water and woods lived supremely oblivious, above our love and beyond our care.

Or we cherish them because they're beautiful, black, white and red—that uncanny red eye set in shining jet. Or it's the voice, unmistakable and indecipherable, despite efforts to decode it. Or it's a guilty love, because our kind nearly destroyed them, and what we want is atonement.

Or it's all of these and how one bird can evoke an entire place, a landscape that is worth calling upon anywhere, anytime. Like many who regard the Adirondacks as home, the birds are really seasonal residents. They simply can't stay when winter locks the lakes.

Loons make other sounds, not just lunatic laughter and throaty tremolos. The rhythmic beat of wings—how fitting that the long feathers are called remiges, from the Latin word for oars—can be heard on a still, late-fall day, when the birds' voices are mute as they leave us behind. They row through the air, just as they fly under the water. And when the ice is water, months from now, they will return, faithful to their own Adirondacks.

—NOVEMBER/DECEMBER 2006

Trust Company
On the ropes with Adirondack Experience

"YOU MEAN I JUST hang there in the air? Sweet," says Christina, from Chazy. The eleven-year-old carefully pulls back her long hair as a guide helps her wriggle into a climbing harness and plops a helmet on her head. She clips in to ropes, ready to lose contact with the ground. A pair of lines span the canyon, tied off to stout tree trunks. It's a temporary suspension bridge, without a walkway. The Tyrolean traverse makes crossing the Flume, on the West Branch of the Ausable River in Wilmington, part roller coaster, part fitness course and part flying lesson.

Around Christina in the woods, other kids are doing what adolescents do so well: talking about the opposite sex, listening to iPods or ignoring the supervising adults. Discussing nail polish and fashion sense, one ninety-pound girl says to another, "You don't need to wear makeup because none of the boys at your school are cute." Twelve-year-old Jessica, from Tonawanda, volunteers this pronouncement as she waits her turn on the steep brink of the stream. Never mind that Jessica has not visited the school in question nor actually seen the students there. She knows this fact after a few late nights at the Adirondack

Experience (AE) dorm, an old farmhouse on Adirondack Loj Road, outside Lake Placid.

Blaise takes off his headphones for a minute to tune in to the rest of the group. He's fourteen, from Port Henry, and an experienced bobsled driver who has been on the *Today* show as well as in an Imax movie called *Top Speed*. He's been listening to a Yankees game, already in a sit harness and white helmet, as eager to hook up as everyone else. More than most members of the co-ed group, he's comfortable with risk. In Utah, on the 2002 Olympic track, he went eighty-two miles an hour in a four-man bobsled.

After a jubilant Christina finishes her turn, Blaise trots over to the massive hemlock that anchors the course. The guides check his gear, then disconnect him from Earth. He's dangling face up and headfirst from a long rope, cradled by a belt harness and a chest rig; when he's completely off the ground, feet in a sling, he shoots over the river. Gravity sends him downward; from the bottom of the trajectory he has to pull himself hand-over-hand to the other side. After saying hello to Michelle Charleson and Bob Forster, the far-side guides, gravity again works to return him to a spot sixty feet above the frothing, roaring water. On the bank John Marshall, fifty-six, and his son and AE staffer, twenty-nine-year-old Matt, pull with all their might to bounce and swing Blaise from side to side. He flies up, down, left and right, in huge, swooping arcs. The other kids also tug on the rope, screaming and laughing and cheering him on. Everybody hauls mightily to bring him back, and he stops just below a stand of trees, still suspended parallel to the ground. Girls and boys jostle for position, claiming spots in the line. Blaise is king, for a moment. Then it's someone else's turn to strap in for the wild ride.

A hiker walking past this clump of eleven youngsters would think it's some camp group or outing club, missing the couple of white canes on the ground or taking my guide dog for just another yellow Lab. Along the trail, kids are talking excitedly, occasionally reaching out to each other, or they're arguing about different bands. If anything, they're more connected to each other after only a week than most kids off at camp, partly because they have one overriding experience in common. They're blind.

This ten-day program brings kids from all over New York, Connecticut and Vermont to hike, camp, swim, climb ropes and rappel down North Country cliffs. Participants are funded by the New York State Commission for the Blind and other state agencies, so tuition is not a barrier. For fourteen years, AE founder John Marshall and his team of six full-time and six part-time licensed guides, counselors and social workers have cajoled visually impaired young men and women through settings and circumstances that sighted adults would only watch from the sidelines. After all, if you can't see the bottom of the sheer rock wall or that foaming white water, what's there to be afraid of? The trust earned by the AE staff and confidence acquired by the youngsters turn fear into something else, the true spirit of adventure. "Bonds really form here," says John. "Kids, often alone at their schools, suddenly have peers. They're in these new situations together."

For some, though, even crossing a hometown street can be scary. The comfort of staying safe at home, e-mailing friends or watching TV is compelling. The outdoors is huge, complicated, without clear paths for unaccustomed feet. It requires a patient guide to make the woods so many of us take for granted accessible and interesting. If you can't see the beauty of an Adirondack vista, what's the appeal? AE team leaders deal with these questions daily, thanks to training from the Commission for the Blind and the understanding of problems and issues that comes from thirty-four years of working with at-risk youth.

Adirondack Experience started at a Lake Placid residential school for troubled boys in 1973. Using the Adirondacks for outdoor adventures has always been integral to John Marshall's work, regardless of his students. In 1990 AE became a stand-alone program reaching beyond the school, and three years ago acquired nonprofit status. Now AE operates year-round, working with a variety of youth, with three summer sessions for blind kids and two weeks for them in the winter, when cross-country skiing, snowshoeing and ice-climbing are on the agenda.

To a blind person, quiet is fine but boring. The sounds of a bird, unless they're really distinctive like a turkey gobbling or the deafening *rat-a-tat-tat* of a pileated woodpecker, are abstract without the visual anchors. Smells, especially new ones, need explaining. To a city kid, a pine tree smells like Pine-Sol, not the other way around. Unlocking the woods as a special place, helping participants connect, using all their senses, with a very different environment, is one important objective of the program.

"Challenge by choice" is the mantra. "The goal of AE is to provide children with activities that improve self-esteem and confidence, build trust in themselves and others, improve communication skills and help better prepare them for employment and higher education," according to John. There's more than being outside in a beautiful spot; there are hearty meals, plenty of homemade chocolate-chip cookies, foosball games, informal counseling sessions and phone calls home to report on busy days.

There are other goals too. These students, so comfortable with each other as they shoot baskets at the base camp (one bangs on the metal pole so the ball handler can orient to the hoop), may have few peers at home. The ten days in the Adirondacks build respect between kids, and they look out for each other in ways that may be unusual in other places. Lose your backpack? Someone will find it and bring it right to you. Need direction from the porch to the van waiting to take everyone to a new destination? Another youngster will call out, "Walk toward me. There's a hill and then you're on the pavement. The van is straight ahead." Sure, they tease each other, but these boys and girls have become friends, thoughtful and supportive, after sampling new skills and succeeding in unknown territory. Last summer was my second outing with AE's blind campers. My first trek was to a hot, buggy clifftop, where a group of boys waited anxiously to descend 160 feet, rappelling down fixed ropes, led by the voices of guides stationed on the precipice, at a midway point and at the bottom. Some young men froze in terror as they stepped off into space. But John, Bob and the others never lost patience, never forced anyone beyond his limits. Michael, age twelve, totally blind and wearing hearing aids, took the lines and dropped like Spider-Man. At the halfway spot, a guide with a video camera shouted out, "Mike, lean back and wave to me!" He planted his feet, stretched perpendicular to the cliff and yelled, both hands in the air, "Hi, Mom! Hi, Dad!"

I ventured into the abyss too, on August 30, 2006. I left my guide dog sprawled across the legs of a couple of campers; he was blissfully unaware that I was about to soar over a roaring waterfall. I wrestled into all the gear, clipped the carabiners and lay back. I plummeted down, down, until I heard the tumultuous water. Then I stopped, just long enough to begin pulling myself by hand to the opposite bank. I greeted Michelle and Bob, then let my weight carry me back to that thundering spot just above the cataract.

"Ready?" John bellowed.

"Let's go!" I answered.

Kids, guides, everyone on the bitter end of the rope bridge, yanked and pulled to make the line bounce. I put my head back and arms out, trusting the rope and the people hauling on it. I tossed up and down, with that sensation you get on a good swing-set when you've pumped so hard you're almost weightless. Then the chains hiccup and you're free, suspended between Earth and sky. That's one gift from AE. These kids will never drive a car, and riding a bike is limited to being the backseat stoker, not captain, on a tandem. But at least once on a summer day they can fly.

—2007 ANNUAL GUIDE TO THE GREAT OUTDOORS

——Acknowledgments——

The first order of business is thanks to you, the reader, holding this book and turning its pages. You are making the connections between ink and words, eye and brain, sifting through images and deciphering a narrative. Without the reader there is no story, and without the story the writer has nothing. It's a bit like the tree falling in the forest, and in the Adirondacks this happens all the time.

The stories on these pages have come from my seasons and travels here, and like most North Country tales they are not new. All the works in this collection were published in ADIRONDACK LIFE, a forum for which I have been deeply grateful during my twenty years at the magazine.

I am indebted to neighbors who shared old ways, and now that many are gone it's safe to give them the recognition they deserve: Art Gates, Mary Cummins, Alta Johnson, Gerard Arsenault, among others. I don't believe you can embarrass a dead person. I hope their children and grandchildren are proud of them for their generosity and kindness, honesty and humor.

Though stringing words and sentences together is a solitary act, I thank the writers whose research and storytelling I admire and whose friendship and occasional praise have given me the confidence to trust my own voice. The master list is very long but for this material I am grateful to Chris Jerome and her late husband, John; Sally Friedman; Amy Godine; Bill McKibben; Anne Mackinnon; Jane Mackintosh; the late Barbara McMartin; and the late John Mitchell.

Over the years ADIRONDACK LIFE coworkers have been immensely tolerant and supportive. Their myriad talents create a fine publication with lasting appeal. I thank Chris Shaw, Annie Stoltie, Galen Crane, Mary Thill, Kelly Hofschneider, Lisa Bramen, Niki Kourofsky, Janine Sorrell, Kelly Kilgallon, Matt Paul, Jo'el Kramer, Liz Tait, Marty Kilburn, Juanita Johnson, Kim Colby, Linda Bedard, Cyndy Douglas, Marion Zapata, Ann Hough, Lisa Richmond and of course, the key members of the publishing team, Joni Manning and Lisa Lincoln.

My days are inherently darker than yours, if you are seeing these lines, but there is light around me, embodied by Tom, Bear and Oakley. Shine on, boys.